JAMĀL al-DĪN al-AFGHĀNI

JAMĀḶ al-DĪN al-AFGHĀNI

A Muslim Intellectual

ANWAR MOAZZAM

CONCEPT PUBLISHING COMPANY
NEW DELHI

First Published 1984

Anwar **Moazzam** (*b.* 1928-   )

Published by

Naurang Rai
Concept Publishing Company
H-13, Bali Nagar
NEW DELHI-110015 (India)

Printed by

Kiran Mudran Kendra,
Mayapuri, Phase I
NEW DELHI-110064

To

My Father and Mother

Preface

The present work is based on my Ph.D. thesis on Afghani's religious ideas submitted at Aligarh Muslim University in 1963. Since then important data on his life and thought has come to light. Some valuable work has also been done on Afghani during this period, particularly at the Universities and other research centres in Europe and U.S.A., which indicates his growing relevance to the recent trends and political developments in the Muslim world. However, these works are focused mostly on his political activities. Among such studies, two books by Nikki R. Keddie deserve special attention due to their comprehensive coverage of Afghani's political life, based on all published and the available unpublished material including research monographs, leaving little scope for any further research in this regard. The existing works are not much helpful in giving an exact idea of Afghani's theoretical framework, explaining his behaviour as a political strategist and an intellectual. My claim to be different is based on an analysis of various aspects of Afghani's intellectual personality, with a focus on points either not noticed or inadequately evaluated by others.

I owe a special debt to the late Prof. Abdul Aleem, my adviser, who remained a source of inspiration throughout the tenure of my research. I am particularly grateful to Prof. S. Maqbul Ahmad and Prof. Munibur Rahman, who had gone through the original manuscript and offered valuable suggestions. I also acknowledge the constant help I received from Prof. Mahmudul Haq, Prof. Moin Shakir, Prof. Afzal Mohammad and Mr. Mahdi Ansari in giving this work a final shape. My wife, Jeelani Bano, and my son, Ashhar Farhan, with their encouraging presence around, made me treat the preparation of this work more as a creative involvement than a mere mechanical exercise in research.

Hyderabad,
October, 1983

ANWAR MOAZZAM

Abbreviations

Āthār	Qāḍi Muḥammad 'Abd'ul Ghaffār, *Āthār-i-Jamāl al Dīn Afghāni*, Delhi, 1940
Biography	Nikki R. Keddie, *Sayyid Jamal al-Dīn "al-Afghāni", A Political Biography*, London, 1972
Documents	Iraj Afshār and Aṣghar Mahdavi, *Documents inedits concernant Sayyed Jamāl-al-Dīn Afghāni/ Majmū 'eh-yi asnād va madārik-i chāp nashudeh dar bāreh-yi Sayyid Jamāl ad-Dīn Mashhūr bi Afghānī*, Tehran, 1963
H	Syed Jamāl al-Dīn Asadābādi, *Nīchariya, Ḥaqiqat-i-Madhhab-i-Nīchari va Bayān-i-Hāl-i-Nīchariyān*, Tehran, 1303, A.H.
Khāṭirāt, Arabic, Persian	Muḥammad Pāshā al-Makhzūmi, *Khāṭirāt Jamāl al-Dīn al-Afghāni*, (2nd ed.), Damascus, 1965 Persian translation : Murtaḍa Mudarrisi Chahar-dihi, *Khāṭirāt Sayyid Jamāl al-Dīn al-Afghāni*, Tabriz, 1328/1949-50
M	Mirza Luṭfullah Khān Asadābādi, *Maqālāt-i-Jamāliya*, Tehran, 1312 Solar
Mashāhīr	Jurji Zaidān, *Mashāhīr al-Sharq*, Vol, II, 3rd ed., Cairo, 1932
Risālah	Shaikh Muḥammad 'Abduh, *Risālah fi Ibṭāl Madh-hab al-Dahrīyīn wa Bayān Mafāsidihim wa-Iṭhbāt anna al-Dīn Asās al-Madaniya wa'l-Kufr Fasād Al-'Umrān*, Beirut, 1302 A.H./1885 A.D.
Sharh	Mirza Luṭfullah Khān Asadābādi, *Sharḥ-i-Hāl wa Āthār-i Sayyid Jamāl al-Dīn Asadābādi*, Berlin, 1304 A.H./1926
SH	W.S. Blunt, *Secret History of the English Occupation of Egypt*, London, 1907
Ta'rīkh	Maḥammad Rashīd Riḍā *Ta'rīkh al-Ustādh al-Imām al-Shaikh Muḥammad 'Abduh*, Egypt, Vol. I, 1931; Vol. 11, 1344, A.H.
TBI	Nāzim al-Islām Kirmāni, *Ta'rīkh Bedāri-i-Irāniyān*, Iran, n.d.
'Urwah	*Al-'Urwah al-Wuthqā*, Beirut, 1328, A.H.
Zu'amā	Aḥmad Amīn, *Zu'amā al-Iṣlāḥ fi Miṣr al-Ḥadīth*, Cairo, 1948

Contents

Introduction

The recent revolutionary developments taking place in the Muslim lands in the form of demolition of monarchies, strong winds blowing in favour of establishment of the rule of *Shari'a* and the non-apologetic and confident assertions of Muslim intellectuals regarding Islam being a functioning modern system of life, might have bewildered many an observer; particularly the western scholars of the traditional orientalist training. These arrogant "outsiders" have almost written off Islam as a spiritual force and material system capable of coping with 'change', a process known as modernisation—a term which ultimately amounts to adoption of Western cultural values and world-view. It is arrogance since it arbitrarily brushes aside any definition of a value-system other than their own. The East still continues to be the White man's burden, now borne by the Western experts and intellectuals.

However, for the Muslims themselves these developments are not new but inherent in the Islamic system itself. For them, with its few but most potent unchanging values, Islam provides for the maximum scope of creative activity in time. It is a mistake, committed by the non-Muslim observers generally, to ascribe the comparative economic and intellectual backwardness of Muslims to the 'dogma' of Islam. To be sure, Muslim civilization achieved its full material prosperity and intellectual brilliance during the medieval period when the Muslims were undoubtedly much more attached to their faith than they were later. The reasons of Muslim cultural decline lie somewhere else and are to be investigated more by economists, sociologists and other social scientists than researchers of religion, as such. One common factor, however, underlying the process of decay of all civilisations seems to be the transformation of their central ideology, Islam in the case of Muslims, into a power-structure (State) with its social, cultural and economic ramifications. This transformation is apparently a logical consequence of the desire of creating a society based on that ideology. Nevertheless, ideology always loses some of its essential features while passing through the process of such transformation. This has happened with Islam also when it was gradually relegated to background by the state which became its own objective. Secondly, the abstract ideology itself cannot guarantee the 'progress' of a people unless it creates a culture through knowledge. Like the modern Western culture, the medieval Muslim culture was based on sciences developed by the Muslims after their mastery over most of the Hellenic, Persian and Indian scientific heritage, without any hindrance from Islamic faith. However, with the degeneration of state from a culture-promoting agency into a self-perpetuating system, knowledge lost its predominant status in culture. Muslim state after detaching itself from Islamic faith and science set in motion the process of decay of society. For its survival, it had to seek alternate sources of power which were available in the form of army and religious elite, the '*Ulamā*—a product of the age of decay. While the army protected the existing power-structure, the '*Ulamā* as the custodians (and not creators) of theological (and not all) sciences, preferred either to support it or remain indifferent, ostensibly to arrest the process of political disintegration. However, the transformation of Islam into an empire and knowledge losing its culture-building role, did not mean the death of Islam as such. It remained at the centre of Muslim consciousness giving rise to various philosophical, legal, mystic and theological trends paving the way for the future divisions of Muslims into different sects, mystic orders and schools of law. From about the 8th century of its inception, Islam, the means of acquiring knowledge of life, had itself become the object of knowledge—pure theology. This theology, moreover, was stagnant and not creative.

Thus at the advent of modern age, it was a politically weakened and intellectually dormant Muslim society which suddenly found itself face to face with a mighty West with its power-generating scientific brilliance. It was not the familiar Crusadic confrontation between Christianity and Islam; it was now knowledge versus ignorance. The question was how to deal with this new challenge. The theologians could not come to the rescue. A different kind of guidance was required and it emerged. Muslim societies of 18th and 19th centuries responded to this new situation with a new intellectual leadership which studied it with admirable clarity. It found that in the changed context Islam has to be understood not merely as a theology but more as a working political, economic and social system. This had to be done with reference to the new values of human society and culture emerging out of the tremendous expansion of knowledge in Europe. To perform this task they had first to question the total authority of the medieval theological system over knowledge. The basic features of the new Muslim response, thus, were liberation from the traditional theological totalitarianism and Islamic reconstruction of society in the changed intellectual and cultural context. This response, however, did not represent the Muslim consensus but a minority of Muslim thinkers while the majority consisting of the *'Ulamā* resolutely resisted any shift from what they considered to be the authentic traditional theological positions. To such minority belongs Jamāl al-Dīn al-Afghāni.

Afghani (1838-39—1897) is unique among the Muslim thinkers of the modern age who continues to serve as a source of inspiration for Muslim intellectuals, both conservative and modern, as well as the Muslim political elite of present day, in general. Intellectuals of modern sensibility like Iqbal find in his thought a framework for the reconstruction of religious thought in Islam. In recent history, the hopes of Muslim political and religious elite and their struggle for establishing an Islamic democratic political system and bringing Muslim countries together can be traced back to Afghani's movements of constitutionalism and *Waḥdat al-Islāmia.*

This sustained relevance of his thought is perhaps due to his deep insight into the future (which is our present) and, secondly, to the fact that the socio-political structure and problems of Muslim societies have not changed in essence since his times. During the later half of the 19th century he saw that the nations of the East in general and the Muslims in particular were at the verge of losing their political and cultural identities under the thrust of western imperialism and because of their incapacity to deal with the inroads the western culture (based on modern sciences) was making into their stagnant societies. Afghani was perhaps the first Asian to identify these two elements of the west threatening the very survival of the East. This diagnosis, however, did not imply outright rejection of both. He was shrewd enough to see the relationship between the two. The rich culture and political strength of the west were essentially the product of modern sciences. Therefore, Muslim societies had to react to these two in different ways. The task before them was two-fold—to survive against the immediate threat of imperialism and to re-emerge gradually as a powerful culture. On the political plane, Afghani suggested unity of Muslim states (described by the western political analysts as aggressive Pan-Islam which it was not) and political modernisation as a means to face the designs of western imperialism. On the intellectual plane he emphasised the need to fill the gap between the medieval Muslim and modern western knowledge. However, in view of the immediate threats of European powers and of Russia he was forced to take up the political task first which turned out to remain as his main pre-occupation till his last moments.

Compared with the wide range of Afghani's vision, the understanding and response of the conservative and enlightened Muslim elite of his period exhibited no insight into the real nature and proportions of the problems. There was no intellectual in the Muslim world equal to the task of meeting the emerging complex challenges except Sir Syed Ahmad Khan, Amir Ali and Chiragh Ali of India. For any guidance the Muslim masses had to look up to the religious elite which could do nothing except to fall back upon the traditional theology and reassert its known positions. Against western imperialism, the *'Ulamā* in different countries reacted in different ways; while the Indian *'Ulamā* resisted British take-over of India (*Taḥrīk-e-Mujāhidīn*) those in Turkey and Iran did not appear to be much concerned with the external potential dangers. With regard to political modernization within, the Indian *'Ulamā* were understandably indifferent. The Iranian *'Ulamā*, however, were fully alive to and opposed the unpatriotic moves by Nāsiruddīn Shah of granting concessions to foreigners for establishment of banks, building railways and telegraph lines, etc. The Turkish *'Ulamā* did not show any opposition to the Sultan/Caliph Abdul Hamid II whose dictatorial regime had, in any case, suppressed all freedom. Notwithstanding their differences in political policies, all the *'Ulamā* with negligible exceptions, were one in rejecting the western sciences and education as harmful on religious grounds. Among the Muslim modernists, none appears to be thinking on the lines of Afghani's three point programme of (i) defence against western imperialism through Muslim unity, (ii) internal political modernisation through establishment of constitutional governments, and (iii) religio-intellectual modernisation. Only the Young Turks seem to be working, independent of Afghani's influence, for political and intellectual modernisation. Among his contemporaries it is only Sir Syed who could match the daring ingenuity of Afghani. Compared with that of Sir Syed, Afghani's thought was more wide-ranging. Sir Syed, after experiencing a bitter counter-attack from the conservatives against his overzealous adventure into rationalization of Islamic metaphysics, confined himself to socio-economic rehabilitation of Indian Muslims as his ultimate objective (a reasonable one in the given situation). Afghani, however, aimed at laying the foundations of an altogether new structure of Muslim society infused with the spirit of philosophy and science through concrete political measures. Although they differed in their objectives, they agreed on the basic defect of Muslim societies—intellectual stagnation. The success and failure of the two varied in nature and extent. Sir Syed failed in his attempt of religious modernisation to a large extent but succeeded in leading the Indian Muslims in the direction of accommodation with social and economic changes through political cooperation with the Indian British government and popularisation of modern education. Afghani, on the other hand, failed in achieving concrete results during his lifetime in the political sphere but was successful posthumously in establishing the anti-imperialist constitutional movements and the religio-intellectual modernisation trends in the Muslim world of the 20th century. In both the cases the decisive factor underlying success or failure was acceptance or rejection of compromise with the authority—political or ideological. Sir Syed's partial success in the educational and socio-political spheres was due to his compromise with the British and his failure in religious modernism lies in his refusal to surrender his right of independent investigation into Islamic theology. Afghani's failure in gaining concrete results was due to his total rejection of any compromise either with imperialism and despotism or conservatism. Nevertheless, both continue to serve as relevant frames of reference for Muslims in various regions of the world. Afghani's views with their focus on almost all vital issues of change attract greater attention.

Afghani, indeed, serves as a model Muslim intellectual for the study of Muslim response to change. He has been studied by the western analysts primarily as a political agitator. For the Muslims he was much more than that. No systematic study of his intellectual personality has yet been attempted, firstly because unlike that of his contemporaries his written contribution in quantity is less and, secondly, his aggressive Islamic political campaigns have overshadowed his more enduring aspects of thought. In fact, his writings and the views recorded by his disciples and companions contain rich data which not only gives an insight into his political campaigns, but, what is more important, also provides the broad intellectual framework which he offered for the urgently needed redefining of the relationship between Islam and the changing world.

The present work is an attempt to reconstruct the framework.

ONE

ON RELIGION

At the outset, it is to be stated that religious reform has no place in Islam unless it is defined as reestablishment of supremacy of the fundamental beliefs of Islam. This implies, firstly, identification of such beliefs and, secondly, deletion of those acquired beliefs and practices which do not agree with the former. Between the two, identification of the fundamentals of Islam, through the process of reinterpretation, has always been the subject of Muslim theologians, jurists, philosophers and the mystics. All the sects, schools of law and philosophy and the Sufi orders are, in a way, the product of such attempts at Islamic reinterpretations. Subsequent to formation of sects and schools of thought during the medieval period, any new attempt of reinterpretation by a thinker is expected to be characterised in relation to the sect or school to which he belonged. However, attempting to reinterpret Islam while belonging to any particular sect or school seems to be self-defeating, since the latter assumes prior acceptance of a certain set of beliefs as essential and, therefore, leaves the former superfluous. Thus, Islamic reinterpretation can be meaningful only when it is independent, but not necessarily exclusive of traditional belief-systems.

Afghani represents such a meaningful attempt of Islamic reinterpretation. His own religious faith cannot be defined in terms of affiliation to any sect or school. The conflicting claims by his biographers and commentators regarding his birth-place being in the Shi'ite Iran or the Sunnite Afghanistan neither intend to prove nor necessarily lead to the conclusion that he was a Shi'a or a Sunni Muslim.[1] He himself has not made any statement in this regard. His closest disciple, Muḥammad 'Abduh' describes him as the follower of the Hanafite school,[2] and W. S. Blunt, recalling a conversation with him, states that his family was Arabian and had always preserved the tradition of Arabic language which Afghani spoke with perfect fluency.[3]

This much is certain that he had studied the traditional Islamic sciences as well as works on Islamic philosophy and Sufism covering areas bordering upon what is described as heretical literature. He was interested, on the one hand, in Muslim rationalists like Ibn Sīnā (on whom he delivered lectures in Egypt) and, on the other, in the Shaikhi school of late 18th century, a philosophical mystical off-shoot of the Twelver Shi'ism, considered to be heretical.[4] His mind was open to all sources of knowledge without any prejudices which take a strong hold on the mind of a reformer intending to study Islamic theology in order to use it for achieving concrete results. It is amply evident that he embarked on his academic career not merely as a student of Islamic theology but more as a thinker-reformer, critically examining every school of thought in the context of contemporary situation and knowledge. However, according to his own admission, his search proved futile and ultimately he returned to the Prophet and his Companions. "I saw that this world was only an unreal mirage and appearance. Its power was precarious and its sufferings unlimited, hiding a venom in every delight, an anger in every benefit. Thus I was inevitably led to remove myself from these tumults and to break all my ties of attachment. And thanks to God and all those who were near Him, I was saved from the world of shadows and penetrated the universe of devotion, resting on the sweetness of the cradle of lights. Today I have chosen for company the Prophet and his Companions."[5]

Whatever his religious affiliations might have been, he himself avoided to be associated with any particular school and preferred to be called simply a Muslim, following different schools on different issues.[6] This doctrinal freedom may be compared, to a certain extent, with the attitude of the Sufis towards matters concerning religion. In fact, Afghani has been described as being somewhat inclined towards Sufism.[7] Yet, apart from this eclectic outlook Afghani's life reflects hardly any of those traits which are traditionally associated with the Sufis, such as asceticism (*ruhbānīyat*), or contentment (*qinā'at*), or self-mortification (*riyāḍat*). Indeed, he was critical of the practices of the Sufis and ascribed the fast spreading inertia among the Muslims to their ascetic teachings.[8] He accused the Sufis of his day of neglecting the true tradition of Sufism initiated by such figures as Bāyazīd, Junaid and Ḥasan of Baṣra, whose piety could not be questioned.[9] Against the prevalent view that one should be content merely with the minimum necessities of life, he gave preference to the idea that all good and desirable things belong to man and should be coveted by him.[10] He pointed out that according to the Qur'an, Traditions and views of the early jurists, religious progress was dependent upon the temporal uplift of the Muslims. Spirituality was no doubt desirable but it could not progress without matter.[11] A nation without political and material strength could not protect its religious character and traditions.[12] Afghani's worldly outlook is more vividly expressed in his remark: "The world is a game of chess; the loser loses and the winner wins."[13]

This approach of Afghani stemmed from his deep faith in rationalism. All available sources show that his education was not confined to religious sciences only. Together with the study of Muslim sciences, he had mastered philosophy, physics, metaphysics, mathematics, astronomy, medicine, anatomy, etc. Besides, he seems to have been familiar with European sciences and their methods,[14] though apparently he did not have a deep understanding of these. He had studied Greek philosophy through Arabic translations.[15] He stands conspicuous among the '*Ulamā* of his time for his unprejudiced understanding of the proper functions of different sciences and their relation with each other.[16] He firmly believed in the evolutionary process of development of human knowledge. He admitted that modern sciences were far ahead of those known to early Muslim scholars.[17] Without denying the necessity of studying early doctors Afghani warned against developing a prejudice towards modern sciences. Citing al-Ghazāli in support of his view, he refuted the idea prevalent among the Muslims that modern sciences were harmful to Islam as a religion.[18] He held that Islam was not against scientific truths. In case there appeared any incompatibility between the two it was essential to interpret religious principles in order to remove the contradiction.[19] Rashīd Riḍā states: "His method of reading the ancient Arabic works was very different from that of al-Azhar. He would often explain the meaning of a point under discussion until it became clear to the understanding, then he would read the statement of the book and apply it to the point in question; if it was applicable, well; if not, he pointed out what was lacking in it. Or he would read the statement of the book and examine its arguments, and either establish it or disprove it and establish a different conclusion. In this way he would proceed until he had given his own decision regarding matters discussed and was not satisfied merely with an understanding of the book and acceptance of the opinions of the writer."[20] Following this pattern, Afghani studied the early scholars of Islam. His students were so much inspired by his boldness that his critical treatment of the commentaries, even those of Abū Ḥanīfa, were accepted by them without protest.[21] Dogma and philosophy—age-old rivals in the history of Muslim thought—seemed to co-exist in Afghani's mind. He regarded philosophy as the most comprehensive of all sciences and, therefore, pre-eminently essential for building up the character of a nation.[22] To make religion an effective means of moral reform, he attempted to place it on the stable foundations of philosophy.

Dīn

Afghani defines religion as a system of principles constituted by God and preached and taught by man. It reaches human mind through the agency of prophets, who are the recipients of revelation (*waḥī*), while others learn its principles by acquisition and education.[23] Describing man's mind as a clean slate during the early part of his life, he states that the first impression which it receives is that of religion. All other aptitudes and habits acquired by him in his later years are influenced by religion.[24]

The nature of this primary influence, asserted by Afghani, is ethical. Even if a man forsakes his religion he cannot possibly abandon the moral qualities and dispositions which religion has already created in him.[25] Afghani stresses the social aspect of religion. He says that the criterion for judging moral and social values is the extent to which they help in creating a balanced society and claims that religion serves as a basis for all such values.[26]

Afghani studies man primarily as a psychic being governed by instincts, desires and ambitions. Man, naturally, aims at the satisfaction of instincts, but, according to Afghani, every individual is not entitled to this freedom in view of the fact that conflicts may arise in society leading to its disintegration if man is left to pursue his desires for his own benefit. It is, therefore, necessary to find out suitable ways and means to keep human desires and ambitions within reasonable limits. Afghani thinks that there are four possible ways through which this object could be achieved: force, moral discipline, state authority, and religious faith. As discussed separately,[27] he holds that the first three methods are ineffective, since force creates chaos, moral values are only relative, and state, in most cases, is controlled by undesirable elements. It is only religious faith that can fulfil the function of controlling human actions for social good. He emphasises that belief in God and faith in reward and punishment can control human desires, safeguard human rights, maintain balance in society and serve as a basis for social and cultural attainments. Only a firm conviction in these beliefs makes a man act virtuously and restrains him from vices. A man without religious faith would not be attracted towards such qualities as cooperation, sympathy, and understanding which are essential for the proper functioning of society.[28] Thus, Afghani ascribes to religion a moral code which aims, chiefly, at social good.

Since early times, Afghani points out, man has acquired three beliefs and an equal number of traits on account of religion.[29] The beliefs are: that he is the noblest of all creatures, that his people are superior to other peoples and that he has been created to acquire excellences of a suitable nature which could elevate him to a higher and nobler world. Likewise the three traits are *Ḥayā* (modesty), *Amānat* (trust) and *Ṣadāqat* (sincerity). These beliefs and traits endowed by religion demand that a person should attain higher degrees of excellence in the field of social relations and cultural achievements.

Islam

It will be seen from the foregoing account that Afghani considers religion as an effective medium for the reform of individual conduct and the establishment of a balanced society. In his opinion

Islam possesses all the necessary qualities to perform this function. It does not recognize any union based upon tribe, colour or race. The only unifying link among the Muslims is that of *Ukhuwwa* (brotherhood).[30] Afghani states that Islam not only calls men towards truth and raises them spiritually, but it also explains the principles concerning social relations and individual rights.[31] Islamic teachings are not confined to matters related to life after death, they also pay full attention to worldly existence. It is for this reason that the *Shari'a* provides for *Sa'ādat al-Dārain* (happiness of the two worlds).[32] Afghani lays down the following conditions for the moral, social and cultural uplift of a people and states that these conditions are fully satisfied by Islam. First, that people's minds should be purified of all false beliefs and superstitions; secondly, that human souls should attain high standards of nobility; thirdly, that the articles of faith should be based upon strong rational grounds, superstition should be avoided, and *taqlīd* (blind following of one's ancestors) should not be the sole criterion of one's actions; fourthly, that among every people there should be two groups, one to educate their fellowmen and the other to propagate justice and moderation and to explain the benefits of good conduct and the harms of wrong deeds.[33]

According to Afghani, *Tawḥīd* (belief in the unity of God) enjoined by Islam dispels all false notions produced by the practice of worshipping several deities. It also discards such superstitions as the ideas of incarnation and suffering of the deity, which are found in many of the existing religions like Christianity, Brahmanism and Zoroastrianism.[34] These superstitions, in his view, stand between man and reality, paralyze intellect, produce all kinds of moral weaknesses like fear and cowardice, and prevent man from achieving excellence and happiness.[35] Afghani points out that man should have confidence in his capacity and should strive to attain the highest level of nobility except prophethood which God confers upon whomsoever He wills. Such confidence would inspire men to compete among themselves in performing noble deeds and achieving perfection. Without such faith in himself man would feel inferior to others, intellectually and morally. Islam has provided full scope to all human beings, without any discrimination, for achieving nobility and happiness. Not bound by national and sectarian considerations, Islam regards spiritual and mental perfection as the only standard of nobility and superiority. On the other hand, religions, like Brahmanism, base nobility on the principle of caste—a concept which, in Afghani's view, obstructed the progress of its followers in scientific, cultural and industrial fields. Again, according to the Old Testament only the Jews were noble. This superiority was later assumed by the Christian priests who became the sole repositories of nobility. It was only after the weakening of the belief in the superiority of Christian priesthood that European civilization really began to progress. In this respect, Afghani describes Martin Luther as following the example of Muslims.[36] Quoting Guizot's *History of Civilization in Modern Europe*,[37] he argues that the secret of Europe's progress was the appearance of a religious group (i.e. the Protestants) that claimed for itself the right of rational investigation into the Christian beliefs, while the priests insisted that subscribing to authority was the essential basis of religion.[38] It was Luther who led Europe from the state of barbarism to that of civilization. Due to this religious movement the Europeans (Christians) revolted against the Church. Afghani believes that the theological rivalry between Catholicism and Protestantism led to a struggle for progress which produced modern civilization.[39] In contrast to other religions, Islam condemns superstition, rejects *taqlīd* and allows religious beliefs to be examined by reason. It declares that reason is the key to happiness and wrong actions are the outcome of irrational thinking. Other religions lack the quality of subjecting dogma to rational investigation. For instance, the doctrine of Trinity as found in Christianity cannot stand rational scrutiny. The dogmas of Brahmanism are also irrational. Afghani further states that there should be an authority to 'command the good and forbid the evil' (*Amr bi'l-Ma'rūf wa Nahy 'an al-Munkar*) and that among all religions only Islam provides such an authority.[40] Nevertheless, Afghani finds certain common elements in Islam, Christianity and Judaism which have the same origin and objectives complementing each other. Whatever differences appear to exist they are among their leaders and not in their sacred books.[41] In his opinion the perfect religion would consist of the basic truth in these three faiths.[42] It is true that the Christian concept of Trinity goes against the Judaic and Islamic monotheism. In order to remove such external contradictions he suggests the method of *tā'wīl.* He holds that sometimes the inner meaning of Qur'anic verse is different from the external meaning—a distinction which is known by the Sufis. All the three religions are one, at least, on the fundamental concept of monotheism (*Tawḥīd*) and action for the good of man (*Khair al-Insān*).[43]

The Qur'an

Afghani holds that the Qur'an was revealed to the Prophet for the guidance of humanity. It is the Book of Allah, revealed in the simple and easy language spoken by the Arabs. It is unaltered and will remain so for ever to guide the peoples.[44] He regards the Qur'an as representing the highest form of human culture and the true path towards happiness. This holy code is the culmination of the best teachings of all true religions and provides a categorical proof that Islam was the final religion.[45] Afghani analyses the contents of the Qur'an in the following manner:

The Qur'an contains foremost the belief in the Unity of God. Further, it enjoins obedience to the prophets who are the custodians of wisdom. Ignorance and superstitions are condemned and knowledge and wisdom are highly praised. In some verses the harms of sinful actions and the benefits of virtuous conduct have been explained. Citing the examples of the preceding communities, the rewards of righteousness and moderation have been emphasised as well as the punishments of sinful life. In addition, the Qur'an has elaborated the basic principles governing mundane life leading to absolute happiness (*Sa'ādat-i-Muṭlaqa*), and the sufferings brought about by tyranny which is the result of barbarism. It disapproves asceticism and states that whatever is created on earth is for man. All the pleasures of life are the gift of God which should be enjoyed with justice and moderation. World domination is promised to those who have attained perfection rationally and spiritually. As a whole, the Qur'an through its ordinances sows the seeds of wisdom in human existence.[46] When Afghani was asked by Mirzā Luṭfullāh to say something for his guidance in material and spiritual life, he advised, "Read the Qur'an and act upon its commands."[47]

Afghani expresses sorrow at the lack of interest shown by the Muslims in the Qur'an, which did not receive even as much attention as the verses of Sa'dī and Ḥāfiz.[48] He points out that it was the teachings of the Qur'an which revolutionized the life of the Arabs. The Arabs, before Islam, were far removed from a civilized way of life, they were engulfed in ignorance and barbarism, and except poetry, that too full of fanciful thoughts, they had no literature or sciences whatsoever. The influence of the Qur'an manifested itself in the complete transformation of Arab life from ignorance to wisdom and from barbarism to civilization. The Arabs began to realize that their needs could be fulfilled only by attaining social, rational and spiritual perfection. It was due to Qur'anic teachings that the Muslims developed a taste and love for knowledge. To satisfy their thirst for knowledge they did not hesitate to become disciples even of heretics like the Christians, Jews and Zoroastrians, and translated works from Persian, Syriac and Greek into the Arabic language.[49]

Thus, Afghani emphasizes that aspect of Qur'anic teachings which deals, mainly, with the intellectual and cultural uplift of human life. In his writings he quotes particularly those verses which urge upon the Muslim people to adopt a rational attitude towards life, acquire knowledge, and consolidate their social and political position.

Tafsīr

Afghani's ideas on *tafsīr* place him among those later reformers who, conscious of the changed conditions, felt the need of a fresh interpretation of Qur'anic teachings. The exegeses written by the early scholars dealt mainly with the literary or philosophical interpretations of Qur'anic verses. For instance, the *tafsīr* of al-Ṭabari (9th century A.D.) is mainly a source of material for traditional exegeses, al-Zamakhshari's *al-Kashshāf* (11th century), having Mu'tazilite bias, was devoted specially to the lexicographical aspect of the Qur'an, al-Rāzi's *al-Tafsīr al-Kabīr* (12th century) is chiefly an exposition of his own philosophical views and al-Baiḍāwi's *Anwār al-Tanzīl wa Asrār al-Ta'wīl* (13th century) follows, in a comprehensive way, the methods of his predecessors.

Afghani held that the existing *tafsīr* literature was not of much help to the Muslims in view of the changed social and cultural context. He suggests that there is need for a *tafsīr* written with a rational and literary approach taking into account, at the same time, Islamic polity, principles of sociology and anthropology and the means through which the happiness of both the worlds could be achieved.[50] In the context of Western values of socio-political reforms he says that "the true spirit of the Koran is in perfect accordance with modern liberties. Disorders and fanaticism have come from additions and ignorant commentaries. Now the progress of time has shown the evil effects of past mistakes, therefore a learned Mussalman, well acquainted with the liberal principles of Europe, can easily convey them to his people with the authority of the Koran, without difficulties which surround Luther."[51] There is no difference of opinion among the Sunnis and the Shi'as on this account.[52] Afghani draws attention to the Qur'an's emphasis on the need of rational understanding of some of the problems of life. This explains why the pre-Islamic uncultured Arabs, after the advent of the Qur'an, came to dominate the world of politics as well as of science.[53]

His views on the preparation of a fresh commentary are more vividly expressed in his criticism of the *Tafsīr al-Qur'ān* written by Syed Ahmad Khan.[54] He suggests that a fresh *tafsīr* should be prepared after an exhaustive study of all the *tafsīrs* written earlier by the traditionists, jurists, scholasticians, philosophers, mystics, men of letters, logicians and even heretics like Ibn Rāwandi. The author of such a commentary must be well-versed in both Eastern and Western sciences. This commentary should contain rational arguments proving the need of religion for humanity. It should deal with influences of religion upon human society and people's minds and should survey the common points among world religions as well as their points of difference. It should also give a new interpretation to the Divine polity and Qur'anic morality which unified the Arabs in the midst of barbarism and disintegration, purified their thoughts and minds and elevated them among the nations of the world. All such matters dealing with the manners of life, good conduct and principles which aim at maintaining a balance in the social and cultural life should be discussed fully.[55]

Afghani is not prepared to extend the scope of interpretation to all fields of human activities. He draws a line between matters relating to the intellectual pursuits of man, on the one hand, and the moral and social reforms, on the other; the latter being the mission of a prophet. He criticizes the prevalent trend among the '*Ulamā* of attempting to prove that all modern scientific theories and inventions have been mentioned in the Qur'an. He regrets that the real message of the Qur'an is lost amidst a host of misinterpretations. So far as the scientific discoveries are concerned, the Qur'an cannot deny them. Neither one should expect to find reference to modern scientific inventions in the Qur'an, like railways or electricity. Had there been any such references the people of that period would have considered them as lies. If there appears to exist any contradiction between the Qur'an and scientific discoveries and concepts it has to be removed by recourse to *ta'wīl.*[56] The Qur'an, in a way, contains indications of later scientific discoveries; for instance, Soloman's use of winds to carry his commands and of lightening to take his messages, anticipate modern inventions like aeroplanes and telegraph.[57] Similarly, there are certain subtle references in the Qur'an to roundness of earth, its rotation on its own axis and around the sun and the sun and earth having been one in distant past.[58] On the other hand, there are clear and specific norms and values underlying social and political organization like consultative government (*uṣūl al-ḥukūmat al-shūrawīyah*), duties of rulers and discussing problems with the peoples. For instance, the Surah *al-Nimal* (the Ant) mentions Queen Sheba consulting people's assembly while confronting King Soloman and the people promising to fight if she declares war against Soloman.[59] The Qur'an, again, gives instructions regarding economic life dealing with issues like taxation, wealth, etc., which can be useful for the modern societies.[60] Afghani also criticizes rationalists who go to the extent of denying the existence of such phenomena as Angels, Jinn, Heaven and Hell and treat them only as symbols for something else.[61] He prefers to accept such beings in their literal sense.

'*Aqīdah* (Belief)

The subject of religious belief has received considerable attention of Afghani. He holds that beliefs which get engraved in human hearts have great influence in determining man's actions, which in their turn produce other beliefs.[62] The close relationship between belief and action makes it necessary to have good beliefs so that good actions may be produced. The brotherhood and unity of

Muslims derive their strength from the beliefs held commonly by them.[63] To determine the soundness of beliefs they should be examined rationally, but this does not exclude other ways of judgement. Afghani observes that the test of beliefs is their capacity to help in material progress. He holds that there is no harm in having beliefs, whether rational or irrational, as long as they do not directly come into conflict with social progress. In fact, no religion has ever enjoined beliefs which prevent material prosperity.[64] In support of his contention he refers to the accounts of the Hindus, Egyptians, Chaldeans, Greeks, Persians, Christians and the Arabs and points out that all these nations reached the peak of cultural and scientific progress notwithstanding their faith in numerous deities and most irrational notions.[65]

An interesting theory is offered by Afghani with regard to the philosophical justification of interpretation of religious beliefs in relation to cultural progress of a nation. In his hard-hitting criticism of the *tafsīr* of Sir Syed[66] he wonders why Sir Syed, who claimed that the purpose of his writing the *tafsīr* was reformation of Muslims, should have attempted to eradicate Muslim beliefs at a time when all other religions had started a campaign of degrading Islam. "Does he not understand that if the Muslims with their weakness and chaotic conditions cease believing in miracles of the fire (of hell) and regard the Prophet as (merely a leader like) Gladstone, they would certainly detach themselves from (their) weak and dominated group and join with the strong dominating group (of the ruling Christian community), since in the prevailing conditions there is no restraining factor and no fear (from doing so). Demands for change of religion, looked at from another angle, are very much present since everyone is always inclined to adopt the appearance and way of life of the dominating (group)." Further, discussing the relationship between religious beliefs and cultural progress, Afghani states that Sir Syed appears to hold that such beliefs are mainly responsible for the decay of the Muslims and if these are eradicated they would regain their past glory and honour. "I pondered (over this view) and said to myself that the Jews by the grace of these very beliefs liberated themselves from the servitude of the Pharaohs and attained power and culture. The Arabs, by virtue of the same, rose from the land of Arabia and flourished in the world in power, culture, knowledge, arts, crafts, trade and commerce. The Europeans recognized these believing Arabs as their teachers. The Hindus during the era of their progress in the laws of culture, sciences and various branches of arts, had belief in thousands of *avatārs*, ghosts, deities, demons and Hanuman. The Egyptians while believing in deities, cows and cats, laid the foundations of culture, sciences and arts and became the teachers of the Greeks. The Chaldeans while worshipping the stars were establishing observatories, making astronomical instruments, building huge palaces and writing books on crafts. The Phoenicians, during the period when they engaged themselves in land and sea trade, contributed to arts and conquered the British, Spanish and Greek countries, used to offer their children as sacrifice to their gods." Afghani points out that the Greeks in the days when they were producing great philosophers and intellectuals, believed in all kinds of gods and superstitions. Likewise, the later Christians while believing in Trinity, confession, cross, etc., strengthened their empire, entered into the field of sciences and arts and reached the peaks of culture, and, today, they are the torchbearers in these spheres. The main thrust of Afghani's argument is that "it is not the religious beliefs, whether right or wrong, which are opposed to culture and material progress, but that belief which prohibits learning of sciences, earning one's livelihood and the ways of culture. I do not believe that there is any religion in the world which opposes these things. I would rather say that it is non-believing which inevitably leads to disorder and distortion in culture as in the case of the Nihilists." He points out that had "non-believing" been the cause of the progress of nations, then the Arabs should have achieved success in culture during the days of *Jāhilīya*. The Arabs remained in the state of barbarism because they believed in the way of atheism (*ṭariqa-e-dahriya*). Afghani concludes that by eradication of Muslims' beliefs Sir Syed aimed at serving others and attempting to follow others' approach/ideology. It may be noticed here that Afghani makes a distinction between the rational and cultural values of religious beliefs. The beliefs may be retained with all their irrational elements (if there are any) so long as they do not obstruct cultural advancement. They are, however, liable to rational examination when they tend to prevent material progress.

Bid'a

Bid'a means some view or action which has not been held or practised by the Prophet and which is not in accordance with the basic principles of the faith. This innovation or novelty does not actually reach the point of unbelief (*kufr*). However, since it lacks the sanctity of the Qur'an or the Ḥadīth, Muslim theologians have regarded *bid'a* as damaging to purity of Islamic beliefs. With the expansion of Islam in different lands and among peoples having different cultural backgrounds, such innovations have crept into Islamic concepts and rituals. Afghani often complains that Muslims had ignored the Qur'an and its teachings and had accepted innovations and all kinds of superstitious practices in social life which were most condemnable.[67] He does not see *bid'a* as a revolt against Sunna, but rather as a misapprehension (*ishtibāh*) of sound beliefs. He gives two reasons for which a true belief is transformed into *bid'a*; firstly, when a principle or belief relating to human good and perfection is propounded, those who are newly converted to Islam might fail to grasp the true spirit of this principle and interpret it in a way not in conformity with the *Shari'a*; secondly, such converts might already be in possession of some false notions which might be confused with newly acquired doctrines of Islam, thus producing an altered or altogether new belief. In both the cases the true belief is distorted and takes a shape quite different to what it originally was. Due to this confusion one distorted belief goes on to create other beliefs equally false. Throughout this process the believer has no idea how the confusion takes place and how beliefs can be purified. Consequently, the people having superficial knowledge ascribe the harmful effects to the original doctrines whereas they are, in fact, the outcome of distortions.

In most cases this deviation from faith and submission to innovations serve as a basis for corrupting people's characters and their actions. The ignorant observers condemn Islam and its true beliefs in the name of such innovation and cite the examples of those persons who believe in innovations rather than in true doctrines.[68]

Ijtihād

As referred to above,[69] Afghani was not prepared to be bound by the decisions and opinions of the early *'Ulamā* and jurists. This attitude is significant since it was a revolt against the most revered authority of the early masters of theology, whose words had acquired almost the same sanctity for the Muslims as the commands of the Qur'an.

Afghani declined to regard the laws of Islam laid down by early jurists as unchangeable. He endeavoured to convince the Muslims that "the law of Islam was no dead hand but a system fitted for the changing human needs of every age, and so itself susceptible of change."[70] He taught that Sunnite Islam was capable of adapting itself to all the highest cravings of the human soul and the needs of modern life.[71] He emphasized that Islam should change according to the demands and requirements of every age so that it might be in harmony with the existing conditions; otherwise, there is a danger of its extinction.[72]

Now, how would it be possible to do away with the practice of *taqlīd,* and pave the way for the formulation of principles which, on the one hand, should conform to the Qur'anic text and, on the other, meet the demands of the day? Afghani had a solution. He started by differentiating between the *uṣūl* (roots) and the *furū'* (branches) of the laws. He believed firmly in the former and allowed full freedom for reason to introduce modifications in the latter. [73] As far as the fundamental principles were concerned he admitted their authority. However, the opinions of early teachers were not to be followed necessarily for two reasons. First, such opinions were formed according to the intellectual capacity and knowledge of those *'Ulamā* and, secondly, they were shaped in response to the problems of their own age. However, since then, knowledge had advanced considerably and the existing problems were altogether different from those of the past. Hence, reliance upon the opinions held by the predecessors should be given up.[74]

Discussing the controversial issue of *ijtihād,* Afghani remarks: "The miseries of Islam are due to the despotic Muslim rulers and the *'Ulamā* who interpreted Islam to suit their own purposes . . . Instead of adapting faith to reason and logic they wish that reason and logic should be adapted to faith as conceived by them. . . . They should realize that unless they clothe religion in knowledge they would not be included among civilized and educated peoples."[75]

Afghani had a contempt for *taqlīd* and called for exercising the right of independent judgement. "What does it mean when it is said that the door of *ijtihād* has been closed? By which *naṣṣ* (Qur'anic verse) has it been declared so? Which teacher (*Imām*) has held that it is not correct to employ *ijtihād*, take guidance from the Qur'an and the true traditions (of the Prophet) and formulate principles in accordance with the current sciences and the requirements of the age?"[76] He pointed out that the early '*Ulamā* themselves had exercised the right of independent judgement. But it would be wrong to presume that they had exhausted all the secrets of the Qur'an.[77]

When, during a discussion, an opinion of the distinguished jurist, Qāḍī 'Iyāḍ (478-544 A.H./1085-1149 A.D.) was quoted and over-emphasized by its narrator, Afghani remarked that whatever Qāḍī 'Iyāḍ said was according to his intellect and the needs of his own times. It would be more proper to say something which would be convincing and true rather than cite the opinions of Qāḍī 'Iyāḍ and other teachers. He pointed out that Qāḍī 'Iyāḍ and '*Ulamā* like him allowed themselves to reject the opinions of their predecessors and inferred those principles which suited the demands of their own age. Therefore, asked Afghani, "Why should we not deduce laws which would fulfil the requirements of our own age."[78]

Besides helping in the formulation of laws meeting the demands of the modern age, *ijtihād* is also an effective instrument for purifying religion from false beliefs and corrupt practices indulged in by the *mullās* and represented as true articles of faith. He remarked that "*ijtihād* rediscovers religion by removing superstitions."[79]

To sum up, Afghani regarded Islam as a dynamic religion and not a static one. The jurists of Islam, from time to time, in response to the demands of the age, had exercised their own judgement to deduce laws and principles from the infallible source—the Qur'an and the Ḥadīth, and, likewise, the present age with changed conditions was in need of a new interpretation.

Al-Qaḍa wa'l-Qadar

The views of Afghani on this issue[80] may be regarded as a reply to European criticism of the Muslims which ascribed their backwardness to the belief of *al-Qaḍā wa'l-Qadar.* According to such criticism, this belief was responsible for paralyzing the energies of the Muslims and was the chief cause of their moral degeneration. This doctrine made the Muslims regard all their actions and achievements as dependent on the will of God and, for the same reason, they were unable to safeguard their rights and protect their countries from tyranny—thus obstructing their overall progress.[81]

Afghani set aside this criticism and held that it confused the doctrine of *Qadar* with that of *Jabr.*[82] Explaining the difference between the two, Afghani condemned the doctrine of *jabr*, the deterministic view which reduced man merely to an inanimate being, having no will of his own and no power over his actions. He also condemned the attitude presenting God as a coercive power upon whose will the existence of each and every event depended and which deprived man of the right of choice (*ikhtiyār*) in his actions and thus rendered futile human faculties of thought and action. Such an attitude would rob man of all urges for positive struggle, learning and acquisition, and would make his life useless.[83] Afghani asserted that this conception was held valid by no one among the Muslims whether they be Sunnī, Shi'a, Ismā'īlī, Wahhābī, or Khārijī. On the other hand, Muslims had full faith in the freedom of will and action.[84]

With certain reservations, Afghani accepted both the basic principles of God's omnipotence and human responsibility. He maintains that God is the Creator of the universe, which functions according to fixed natural laws. Events take place in time abiding by the law of causation, the *causa causaus* being God. It is through these natural laws and principles of causation that man is bound to God's will. His knowledge of events is limited to the causes within the range of his perception. Whatever is outside that range, whether in the past or in future, is known only to God.[85]

Explaining the close relationship between nature and human will, Afghani states that human will is produced by perception (*idrāk*) of the external phenomena and it is, in fact, one of the links in the chain of causes. The source of the causes underlying external events is God, who has subordinated each event to a like cause.[86] Thus, Afghani accepts God's power over human will, not directly but through the law of causation.

Now, this situation leads to the question of human responsibility and brings in the issues of *kasb* (acquisition) and *ikhtiyār* (choice). Without making any distinction between the two terms and using both of them in the sense of *ikhtiyār*, he asserts that God has endowed man with full powers of choice over his actions. It is only the right of choice which makes human responsibility just and valid, and as such, man stands responsible to the laws of *Shari'a* for his acts and is liable to reward and punishment.[87]

Thus, Afghani differs slightly from the stand of al-Ash'ari who, while admitting in man a power to act, emphasises that it never in any way passes out of the control of God. Afghani's point of view seems to be closer to the *Māturīdī* stand which holds that God has created in man the power really and not metaphorically.[88] He believes that God's omnipotence is manifested, chiefly, in His being the Master of universe through unalterable laws of nature. He may be called a determinist in the sense that to him human actions cannot escape the effects inherent in natural laws.

The other aspect of his argument is ethical. He maintains that strong faith in law having full power over the events gives strength to human conduct. Belief in *al-Qaḍā wa'l-Qadar* makes man brave, patient, bold, generous and self-sacrificing so that he is prepared to face the circumstances without fear.[89] Again, belief in predetermined death, faith in God as the provider of one's livelihood, and complete trust in an Omnipotent Being gives sufficient courage to fight in defence of truth.[90] He points out that it was in this sense that the early Muslims believed in *al-Qaḍā wa'l-Qadar*. He supports this view by citing the political and cultural triumphs of early Muslims which were brought about, according to him, by a religious momentum generated mostly by this belief.[91]

Besides, this belief does not rest exclusively on religious sanction as such. It is more a rational attitude than a theological dogma. The rule of this law prevailed over all great human achievements wherever they took place. Historical figures like Cyrus, Alexander, Jingiz Khan and Napoleon were the symbols of the spirit of *al-Qaḍā wa'l-Qadar*. Their achievements were due to bravery, courage, optimism, patience, open-heartedness, sacrifice and such other qualities as are inherent in this belief.[92]

Afghani, however, does not deny the fact that some elements

of *jabr* have been introduced in the concept of *al-Qaḍā wa'l-Qadar* by the Muslims consciously or unconsciously. Probably the reason for the backwardness of the Muslims was their faith in absolute determinism. He suggests that this error should be rectified by the *'Ulamā* and the true nature of this belief should be established by the removal of false elements.[93]

Caliphate

For a proper evaluation of Afghani's concept of Caliphate it is necessary to study, first, his views on the Islamic attitude towards the state and the people and the political responsibilities shared by them.

He maintains that Islam recognises no distinction between religion and politics. These two are the branches of the same tree. The Prophet and the first four Caliphs were all religious leaders as well as rulers of the state.[94] He holds that religion and politics are like soul and body and that is why God promises a political reward (i.e., government) for the faithful and the virtuous.[95] In other words, Afghani regarded politics as the material expression of spiritual life. He repeatedly states that in order to succeed, religion must be politically strong,[96] the elements of this strength being unity (*ittiḥād*) and political leadership (*siyāsat*). Discussing the difference between religious and irreligious polity, he remarks that the former leads a nation towards democracy, whereas the latter tends towards despotism. As a proof of this view he cites the election of the first four Caliphs and their advisory councils which guaranteed a true and effective freedom to the common opinion. On the contrary, monarchy openly disregards public opinion and is the chief product of materialist polity. He emphasised that Muslims should strive to bring back the Muslim states to their original democratic pattern so that religious politics is strengthened and the right of free expression is restored.[97]

Islam—A Democracy

Afghani firmly believed that the political structure of Islam was basically democratic. He supports this view by the Qur'anic verses which emphasize the importance of mutual consultation in all transactions. As regards the structure of the state, Islam had imposed strict restrictions upon the controlling body which formulated laws and awarded punishments.[98] He regarded the Caliphate as a perfect democratic institution representative of the community.[99] W. S. Blunt, commenting on this, remarks that Afghani and his followers had always maintained that "the growing absolutism of Mohammadan princes in modern times was contrary to the spirit of Islam, which in its essence was a republic where every Muslim had the right of free speech in its assemblies, and where the authority of the ruler rested on his conformity to the law and on popular approval."[100] Afghani maintained that the government of the Muslims was based, first, upon *Shari'a* and, secondly, upon consensus of opinion (*ijtimā' ārā' al-ummah*).[101] The importance of the latter, he points out, was apparent from the fact that it has been placed on the same level as the divine command.[102] Islam, thus, gave the community the right to participate in state affairs and to control the working of the government as well.[103] By participation he meant that the political and administrative responsibilities of the state should be shared equally by the ruler and the ruled.[104] During his stay in Egypt, Afghani suggested that the people should participate in the government and that a truly constitutional government should be set up. Liberty and freedom were essential for man and were not granted willingly by the ruler to the people; they could be acquired only by force and sacrifice. The wise persons close to the ruler should guide him in the formation of a constitutional government. With popular representation in the government the sufferings of the people would be reduced. Citing the example of Western countries where dictatorships had been changed into democracies, Afghani believed that a democratic government was much suitable for Egypt and, in fact, for all Muslim states of the East.[105]

Afghani hoped that a great personality would appear among the Muslims, govern their states, fulfil the condition of trust, obey a constitution and, ultimately, introduce a democratic form of government.[106] The first step which he seems to suggest for changing the Muslim monarchies into democracies was the formation of constitutional governments. His advocacy for the adoption of a constitution in the Muslim states and the abolition of despotism in Egypt, Persia and Turkey was the most significant aspect of his active political life.

Afghani held that justice could not flourish under despotism.[107] He believed that despotism would ultimately disappear as it was against human nature. Despotism would survive in a country as long as ignorance prevailed among the people. With the spread of knowledge, the first step taken by the Muslims would be to change the government and liberate themselves from the bonds of dictatorship.[108] In an address to the Persian patriots he suggested that the principles of government should be laid down and a strong movement should be launched for the constitution and against despotism. "Law (*qānūn*) should rule over a nation, for, it treats the King and the beggar equally."[109] Afghani refuted the idea that formulation of laws was against Islam. On the contrary, it was through the promulgation of laws and establishment of consultative assemblies (*dār al-shūrā*) that the true doctrine of Islam would gain real strength.[110] Society could flourish only under a constitutional government (*mashrūṭīyat*). Afghani compared the people to plants which were uprooted by the furious wind of despotism and even if they survived they could not bear fruit. On the other hand, law served as a gardener taking proper care of the growing plants according to their nature, helping them to grow stronger and bear fruit. Afghani condemned despotism which was opposed to peoples' progress and individual efforts to attain high distinctions in life. It brought human beings down to the level of animals and took the soul out of a nation in such a way as to leave the body intact but lifeless.[111] Rebuking the Persian people for tolerating the tyranny of despotism in silence, Afghani said, "God created you free but you have imprisoned yourselves. You have put the chains of the tyrant around your own necks."[112] He remarked: "I hate both the oppressor and the oppressed; the oppressor for oppression and the oppressed for tolerating it (without protest)."[113]

In an article written in 1879, he emphasises the benefits of constitutional government "which would set forth its beneficial results and show how those governed by it have been aroused by original human nature and stimulated to emerge from the lowly state of animality, to ascend the highest degree of perfection and to cast off the burden that despotic government lays upon them."[114] Following the classification of states available in the traditional medieval Muslim thought into cruel, oppressive and compassionate governments, Afghani holds that the compassionate government is the best.[115]

The Caliph, according to the *Shari'a*, should be a person who has full knowledge of the laws of *Shari'a*, has the power to execute them and enjoys the support of the community.[116] The status of Caliph should not be achieved on the basis of inheritance, racial or tribal superiority, physical power, or by virtue of one's wealth.[117] A Caliph has no superiority over other Muslims except in the sense that he guides them in safeguarding the *Shari'a* and acts in defence of the community.[118] It was by dint of these qualities that most of the earlier Muslim rulers claimed for themselves Caliphal rights.[119] In a speech delivered on January 11, 1871, in a gathering of the Turkish constitutionalists at Constantinople, he declared that the Caliph, according to the Islamic principles, was the true representative of the whole Muslim community. This right of representation belongs to all Muslims and no single individual could claim the right of deciding the fate of several millions of Muslims simply because he was of royal blood. The Caliph should be elected by general agreement and for his guidance should have an Islamic parliament based on the pattern of the consultative assembly during the time of the first four Caliphs.[120] Naturally, his concept of the Caliphate as a democratic institution could not be compatible with the continuance of despotism in Muslim countries, especially in Egypt, Iran and Turkey. Addressing the Muslim rulers, he stated that Islam was a constitution based on freedom and equality and, hence, the Caliph was like any other Muslim. Referring apparently to the Turkish Sultan he remarked that if religion was the basis of the status enjoyed by him, the Muslim people, who were equally devoted to religion, should be allowed to share the responsibilities of the government. Afghani demanded that the government should obey the command of God and the Prophet.[121] In Egypt, his efforts were directed, chiefly, towards establishing a constitutional Government. When Tawfik became the Khedive, Afghani insisted that he should fulfil his promise of constitutional reforms—an undertaking which he had given before coming to throne—and advised him to give the people a place in the *Shūra* in order to strengthen his throne and the government.[122] In Iran he was more vigorous in his demands for the end of the despotic rule of Nāṣiruddīn Shāh and the inauguration of a constitutional government (*mashrūṭīyat*). In Turkey, he was faced with the twin problem of constitutionalism and Caliphate. He complained that the Caliphate had degenerated into monarchy, which was acting without seeking advice of the people, whereas it should, in fairness, grant democratic liberties demanded by the people. He suggested that the Caliphate should not be confined to a particular dynasty, but should be given a wider popular basis—as a first step towards the establishment of a republic.[123] He firmly believed that in case the existing generation failed to introduce the change, it would inevitably be brought about by its successors. The constitutionalists, he remarked, would finally succeed in bringing the Caliphate-monarchy in line with the true concept of Islamic Caliphate.[124]

However, in view of a lack of sufficient political consciousness among the Muslims, Afghani was fully aware of the possible dangers involved in the introduction of democracy in Muslim countries. He held that as long as Turkey was not capable enough to accept democracy, election of the Caliph from the royal dynasty might be allowed to continue; but he must be guided and advised in state-affairs by an independent advisory council elected with the consent of the people and gradually there would emerge an indirect cooperation between the people and the government.[125]

In brief, Afghani submitted that (a) despotic governments should be replaced by democratic theocracies; (b) constitutional governments should be formed as a preliminary step towards total democracy, and (c) the Caliphate was to be retained. It was the last which received greater attention in his discussion of *al-Waḥdat al-Islāmīya*, commonly known as Pan-Islamism.

Al-Waḥdat Al-Islāmīya

All aspects of Afghani's religious thought ultimately merge into his project for the unity of the Muslims. His views are replete with anxious appeals to the Muslims, to the Muslims rulers, '*Ulamā* and the people to strive for this unity. Quoting profusely from the Qur'an and the Ḥadīth he emphasised that without unity the Muslims could never survive and flourish. The old Islamic principle of *Ukhūwwa* derived from the Qur'anic verse, "*innama al-mu'minūn ikhwatun*" (all Muslims are brethren) was, for the first time, utilized by him for practical political aims. In view of the growing political penetration of the European powers, especially Britain, Afghani called the Muslims to forget their internal rivalries, political and religious, and unite themselves against outside dangers. Declaring that "there is no nationality of Muslims except Islam (*Lā jinsīya li 'l-Muslimīn illā fi dīnihim*),"[126] he reminds his fellow believers that unity (*wifāq*) and power (*ghalb*) are the two chief pillars of Islam.[127] Deriving his inspiration from the verses of the Qur'an and Ḥadīth, he advises the Muslims to come close to each other, remain steadfast on the true path of God and to purge the disruptive elements from amongst them.[128] The Muslims had already passed through the tribal state which was based on the concept of nationality (*jinsīyah*) and adopted religion as the basis of this organisation.[129] Faith in Islam was for him the only basis of Muslim unity. "Islamic society," he states, "stands witness to the fact that Muslims do not recognise unity on the basis of tribe, colour or race. It is only the religious brotherhood which counts. One would observe that as long as the ruler followed the *Shari'a* faithfully, the Arabs did not resent the rule of the Turks, the Persians readily accepted the government of the Arabs and the Indian Muslims that of the Afghans. However, as soon as the ruler disregarded *Shari'a* and acted according to his own wishes, they turned against him and he became worse than a stranger amongst his own people."[130] Hence it is necessary that the Muslim states should unite under the Qur'anic principles to defend themselves from the foreign enemy and turn back the growing tide which had encircled the entire Muslim community. Could the Muslim states and the Muslim peoples rise from the ruins of their glorious past and face the might of the West ? Afghani was confident that it was within the realm of possibility for them to do so. It has happened in history, in Muslim history itself. There were figures like Abū Muslim Khurāsāni whose movement brought about the downfall of the great Umayyad dynasty and Peter the Hermit, who campaigned in Europe and started the Crusades.[131] He was sure that the Muslims could be awakened and fused into an Islamic unity (*ittiḥād-i-Islāmīya*) to face external threat.[132] By 1883 he had come to the conclusion that there were no other alternatives for the Muslim survival and revival except Islamic unity which he termed as *'aṣabīyah*—a term borrowed from Ibn Khaldūn, which was described in the West as "Pan-Islamism". This *'aṣabīyah* or Pan-Islamism he saw in the growing trends among the Muslims for attachment to the' firm bond' (*al-'urwah al-wuthqā*) of the Caliphate of Sultan Abdul Hamid.[133] Britain, according to him, considered the prestige in which the Caliphate of Sultan Abdul Hamid was held throughout the Muslim world as an obstacle in the furtherence of her interests and wanted to destroy the axis of Muslim *'aṣabīyah.*[134] The Ottoman Empire for him was not only a symbol of Islamic unity but also a political means to preserve this unity and was the guardian of the 'eastern peoples.' Its disintegration meant disintegration of Muslim unity and, therefore, it had to be protected.[135]

He further explains his idea of unity among the independent Muslim states in the following words : "I do not mean to plead for the rule of any particular person, as it may perhaps be considered to be difficult. However, I do wish that the command of the Qur'an should prevail over them and the religion of Islam, should serve as a means of their unity."[136] Afghani suggested that each ruler should take all measures for the security of his neighbouring Muslim countries, since their existence depended upon each other.[137] This unity would make it incumbent on all the Muslim states to put up a joint defence with the approval of the Caliph, whenever a member state was attacked by any foreign power.[138] Such a project, in fact, did not mean to replace regional nationalism (*qaumīyat al-quṭr*) by religious nationalism (*qaumīyat al-dīn*). He wanted that each Muslim state should, as an independent entity, unite with the other Muslim states for a single purpose, that is, political liberation.[139] It is to be noted that Afghani has used the word *jinsīya* in his addresses delivered in Egypt, India and Iran, as a concept unifying local peoples for specific purposes—political (against foreign intervention) and cultural (for greater social solidarity). As such, his concept of *jinsīya* acquires a secular character. For instance, in a talk given in Egypt in 1879,[140] he describes "*jinsīya* of the Eastern peoples" as based, not merely on Islam, but on the pre-Islamic Egyptian, Phoenician or Chaldean civilisations. This civilisation was distinguished for its contributions to sciences like mathematics, engineering, philosophy, etc. The Phoenicians developed the art of writing and the Chaldeans the science of astronomy. He advised the Egyptians to establish a '*Ḥizb al-Waṭani*' (Party of Fatherland) which should "protect the rights of your country and will guard its splendour" by highlighting the great contributions made by their forefathers and by comparing them with the present decay and by educating peoples of the country in the contemporary political developments and problems. He appealed for supporting attempts for the establishment of a constitutional government in Egypt.[141] A similar glorification of ancient contribution of a people to knowledge has been resorted to by Afghani in India, with the similar purpose of unification against foreign domination. In a speech delivered in 1882 at Calcutta, he paid high tributes to Indian civilisation—the cradle of humanity—for its historic contribution to world knowledge, particularly to mathematics, geometry, astronomy, law and philosophy.[142] He criticises the obstructive role of the Westerners in the intellectual awakening of Muslims in various countries. During his stay in Istanbul he pointed out[143] that the peoples of the west were more interested in disunity and lethargy among the peoples of the East since it suited the former's political interests. The Easterners have to unite for the protection and progress of their fatherland (*Waṭan*) under the guidance of their brave leaders. The western peoples in order to succeed in their designs are ignoring the eastern languages (like Arabic, Persian, Urdu, Hindi, etc.), culture and education. He points out that there is no community (*Jāmi'a*) without a language, no language without a culture (*adab*), no honour without history and no history for a nation if there is no one to preserve the contribution of their great men. The maintenance of the language, culture and honour of a community depends solely on the education of one's own country (*ta'līm-e-waṭani*) based in one's fatherland for the sake of fatherland, irrespective of religious or other differences among the peoples.[144] Children should be sent to these people's schools which impart patriotic education and teach sciences and technology useful for them.[145] This call for territorial patriotism need not be taken as going against his appeal for *Waḥdat al-Islāmīya* aiming at the unity of all Muslims of various countries on the basis of faith. In fact, in his scheme the territorial unities were essential in order to face the imperialist or dictatorial regimes and designs, as a whole. Thus Pan-Islam and the struggles for local unities were coterminus.

Besides political unity, Afghani laid great stress on close coordination between the *'Ulamā* of Muslim countries. He suggested that the *'Ulamā* of each Muslim country should form organisations which should be united into a central organisation set up at Mecca. This central organisation would, in case of foreign interference, extend to the branches all kinds of help in religious and political matters. The organisations of the *'Ulamā*, besides giving a religious leadership, would also ensure the purity of Islam against innovations. Mosques and Muslim schools, Afghani suggested, should be utilised as educational centres interconnected with each other and ready to respond when the occasion required.[146]

This unity was, of course, to be achieved under the framework of the Caliphate. He was prepared to accept any Muslim ruler as the Caliph provided the Islamic union had its capital at Constantinople. In a talk with W. S. Blunt, he expressed his willingness to accept Mahdi of Sudan, Sharif Muhammad Ibn Aun or the Imam of Yemen as the Caliph.[147]

At this stage, it would be interesting to note that besides a union of Muslim countries, Afghani had also sought to bring Britain or Russia into a pact with the Muslim states. W. S. Blunt records several meetings in London in 1884-1885 between Afghani and Randolph Churchill and Drummond Wolf, during which the question of a British-Muslim alliance was raised. On July 23, 1885, Afghani suggested to Randolph Churchill that Britain must make an alliance with Islam, with the Afghans, the Persians, the Turks, the Egyptians, the Arabs, especially to check the possible Russian advance over Afghanistan and India.[148] However, the talks came to an abrupt end due to lack of interest on the part of the British government. The failure of the talks made him change his plan altogether. He, then, proposed to form "a union of Muslim countries with Russia against British Empire."[149] His anxiety to form the union is apparent from his readiness to accept help from whichever country it could be obtained. Earlier in January, 1885, he and his friends in London, considered another plan, described by Blunt as the Franco-Russo-Indian conspiracy—Afghani as its head.[150] It was decided that if the Sultan did not work with them he would be deposed. By this plan they wanted "to force terms of peace on England, failing which there might be a revolt in India."[151]

Although the above mentioned plans failed to materialise, Afghani never abandoned his efforts for the unity of all Muslim states. His plans for such a unity were advocated most effectively in 1884, through his influential journal *al-'Urwah al-Wuthqā*. Addressing all Muslim rulers, *'Ulamā* and common people he called upon them to form an alliance. He was well aware of the Shi'a-Sunni schism which he took pains to iron out. He repeatedly appealed to Afghanistan and Iran to forget the superficial religious differences and to come closer to one another.[152] Through the *'Urwah* he appealed to Persian journals to popularize especially those ideas which were related to Islamic unity and the restoration of national ties among the Muslims.[153] He reminded the Afghans that they and the Iranians were, in fact, "two branches of the same tree", that is, the ancient Iranian race.[154] He suggested that the Iranian *'Ulamā* and the *Mujtahids* should write articles and pamphlets upon the need of unity among different groups of the Muslims.[155] In 1892, Afghani was invited by Sultan Abdul Hamid II to Constantinople to give shape to his union plan. At the outset, Afghani accepted the Sultan as the Caliph of the proposed union.[156] Firstly, it was argued that negotiations should start at a higher level between Abdul Hamid and the other Muslim rulers including Nāṣiruddīn Shāh of Persia, Khedive of Egypt, and the Sultan of Moracco. Secondly, the chief obstacle to Muslim unity—the Shi'a-Sunni differences should be removed by negotiations with the Shah. Sultan Abdul Hamid is reported to have agreed to Afghani's proposal that as a gesture of good will the territory called *Bain al-Nahrain* (Iraq) in the Turkish Empire which was sacred to the Shi'a community, should be made a part of Iran. Thirdly, a high level organisation should be established at Constantinople and should consist of two representatives from each Muslim country—one, representing that state, and the other, representing the people from among the '*Ulamā*. This central organisation would look after the problems of all Muslim countries and its decisions would be respected unequivocally by everyone.[157] Again, if any European power interfered in the affairs of any Muslim country the organisation would declare *jihād* and prohibit all trade relations with that power.[158]

Armed with the plan, Afghani entered into correspondence with the rulers and '*Ulamā* of the Muslim countries and the response was very encouraging.[159] The letters were addressed to the Shi'a '*Ulamā* of Iran, Iraq, India, the Arab countries, Balkh and Turkestān, requesting them to support the Sultan. It is reported that within six months about (200) favourable replies were received.[160] However, Afghani could not continue his work due to severe opposition by the persons close to the Sultan, who were alarmed by Afghani's increasing influence on him. The Sultan was made suspicious of Afghani's intentions.[161] In fact, there never existed an atmosphere of mutual trust between Afghani and the Sultan. There was a basic difference between the Pan-Islamic conceptions of the two. Afghani aimed at the wider and deeper religious and intellectual renaissance of the Muslims through the removal of the major obstacle of political disunity. On the other hand, the Sultan had supported the Islamic unity project for no other reason than to strengthen his political authority in Asia as the spiritual head of the Muslims. It seems that with the progress of the plan this vital difference in outlook became more apparent. Besides, Afghani's well-known advocacy for a constitutional government might have been another obstacle in their cooperation. The Sultan, as subsequent political developments showed, was in no mood to surrender his despotic rule in favour of a constitutional government. So, the inevitable clash between their ultimate aims made Afghani abandon his work and with that his last hope for the fulfilment of his life mission was lost.

Islam and the West

Afghani, on the one hand, criticizes Western hostility towards Islam in religious and political spheres and, on the other, lays equal emphasis on Islam as a modern and democratic religion. He vigorously attacked European political theories and religious attitudes in comparison with Islamic polity.

Having a firm belief in Islamic democracy,[162] he dismissed the current political theories of the West as incapable of satisfying the needs of human society. He stated that there were three kinds of political systems in Europe : Constitutionalism, which allows a limited freedom to common opinion; Democracy, which gives full representation to common opinion; Socialism, which upholds individual freedom and economic equality. He described Bolshevism and Communism as more developed forms of Socialism.[163]

Commenting upon socialism he admitted that there was in it a tinge of Islamic brotherhood (*ukhūwwa*) since it recognised no distinction of colour and race. However, European thinkers had made the theory of socialism too complex to be understood by the common people. The basis of unity in socialism, that is, economic equality, had no attraction for the people in preference to the system based on religious and cultural affinities. He pointed out that it was an age full of commercial and political rivalries and as long as human society remained divided in this manner no country or people could follow the impracticable principle of economic equality. On the other hand, Islam's basis of unity, that is, *tawḥīd* and belief in Prophet Muhammad, satisfied both the material and the spiritual aspects of human life.[164]

To the idea that Europe aimed at political betterment by means of atheism, Afghani remarked that it was, in fact, inspired by hostility towards Islam. The Christian world had lost its own unity of faith and its sects were not prepared to allow ordinary human rights to one another. The only standard of preference for them was racial superiority. However, the enlightened section of the people was tired of such disruptive ideas and wanted to eradicate the differences of race, colour and religion and desired to establish a world of equality and common brotherhood. Now, there were two ways open for such people, (a) Spiritualism, leading towards true religion and (b) Materialism, culminating in atheism. Following the first path they would perforce arrive at Islam, the upholder of equality and brotherhood. Hence, European politician, not willing to see Islam in a better position, thought it best to direct the minds of the enlightened section towards atheism. Probably, European thinkers regarded atheism less dangerous to Christianity than Islam. In fact, Europe, having no religious spirit, could not be afraid of atheism at all.[165]

Another factor in the European hostility towards Islam was political. According to Afghani's analysis, most of the European powers at that time depended for their existence and progress upon the wealth and production of their Asian colonies.[166] They knew that if Islam succeeded in the West, its democratic teachings would precipitate violent reaction in European circles against their imperialistic and colonial policies and they would have to lose the wealth they were accumulating as wages for their domination over their Asian possessions.[167]

Afghani pointed out that the west was exploiting religion to suit its double-edged policy. Europeans came out as devout Christians whenever they intended to enslave some country. Whereas, when the enslaved nations, acting upon the commands of their religion, rose up for their independence, the same Europeans branded their action as religious fanaticism. In this manner, Europe treated religion not as a means of spiritual betterment, but as a political weapon.[168]

In an article,[169] describing the reasons of Christian supremacy, Afghani discussed the teachings of Islam and Christianity. Holding religious faith as a major factor in moulding human outlook and as the basis of cultural progress, he tried to find out the relation between the teachings of the two religions and the way their followers acted upon them. Christianity, Afghani states, is based on *musālama* (peace), *muyāsara* (gentleness), *raf'al-qiṣāṣ* (giving up retaliation), *iṭṭirah al-mulk wa'l-sulṭah* (casting away power and domination) and asceticism. It advises its followers to obey one who rules over them. They must not take interest in matters concerning the rulers and their possessions and should keep away from personal, national and religious controversies. The statement of the New Testament, "whosoever shall smite thee on thy right cheek turn to him the other also",[170] exhibits the spirit of non-violence in Christianity. In view of these basic doctrines of Christianity Afghani expresses surprise at the conduct and actions of the Christians which were quite contrary to its teachings. He remarks that in practice the Christians were a most world-loving and power-seeking people. There was no limit to their pursuance of the pleasure of mortal life. They occupied distant countries, invented new military weapons, used them against their enemies as well as against each other and concentrated upon organising armies and developing war tactics. Warfare had become almost a science for them. All such activities were not in harmony with the principles of Christianity.

In comparison with Christianity, the basic characteristic of Islam was to struggle for supremacy and to defend itself against any law other than Islam. According to Islam, the Muslims should liberate themselves from any ruler who does not act in accordance with the *Shari'a.* To invent weapons, develop military sciences and acquire such sciences as physics, chemistry and geometry, which help in the mastery of military techniques, are important needs of the Muslims. The fact that the *Shari'a* had prohibited all kinds of betting except on horsemanship and archery (which had military importance) showed that Islam approved of the learning of military arts.

Having explained the fundamental doctrines of the two religions, he enquires why it was that the followers of Christianity, a non-aggressive religion, had surpassed all other peoples in mastering military sciences and were dominating the Muslims whose religion sought power over others. It was the Muslims who used such weapons in the Crusades as were quite unknown to the Christians. Quoting Sir John Malcom's *History of Persia*, he points out that Mahmud of Ghazna used canons during his Indian invasions and defeated the Hindus. In Afghani's opinion, the reason for the rise of the Christians did not lie in their following the teachings of Christianity. It was, in fact, their total disregard for the Christian doctrines which put the Christians on the path of progress. Afghani's analysis of the growth of Christianity is as follows :

He states that Christianity was first embraced by the Romans who, even after their conversion, retained certain beliefs, manners and morals, inherited from their previous faith. Christianity did not impose upon them its new beliefs and laws; instead, it entered into a kind of compromise with their old manners, customs, laws and thoughts. Thus the new teachings did not eradicate the old beliefs. Secondly, in the early period, due to the domination of the clergy, the Bible was not within reach of the common people. It resulted in preventing the propagation of the true teachings of Christianity. The doctrines of Christianity were wrongly interpreted when the Roman Catholic priests, taking upon themselves the function of legislation, provided a religious sanction for the Crusades. At a later stage, a disintegration appeared among the beliefs of the Christians and different sects propagated ideas against the domination of the Church. The Christians reverted to the ideas of their ancestors which were quite contrary to the Christian precepts of peace. Those ideas inspired the Christians with the desire for knowledge. They made a rapid advance in military art as well as other sciences and achieved a prominent position among the peoples of the world.

Contrary to the progress of the Christians which was made by virtue of non-Christian ideas and principles, the early cultural victories of the Muslims were due to their following faithfully the true teachings of Islam. Their disintegration took place when the true principles of Islam were distorted by the admixture of alien influences and beliefs which were held by certain communities converted to Islam. For instance, the doctrine of *jabr* was chiefly responsible for paralyzing Muslim thinking. In the third and the fourth centuries of Hijra heresies emerged. The Sophists propagated the concept that all existence was the product of mere fancy and hallucination. False Traditions were attributed to the Prophet and were mixed up with those which were sound. These false Traditions inflicted a serious blow upon the beliefs, thoughts, and conduct of the Muslims. Besides, the inadequate educational system rendered the '*Ulamā* incapable of carrying the true teachings of *Shari'a* to the common people. In this manner the Muslims lost sight of those principles which might have greatly helped them in their cultural advancement.[171]

In the above analysis, the chief emphasis of Afghani is upon those doctrines which deal with material progress and political consolidation. The progress of the Christians, according to him, was due to their acting upon such doctrines although they did not belong to their religion. The Muslims remained backward because they disregarded these principles which enjoyed religious sanction. Afghani remarks that a nation which accepted Islamic principles consciously or unconsciously was bound to progress. Islam was a religion of action and not merely a jumble of words and terms.[172]

Ishtirākīya (Socialism)

Afghani was fully alive not only to the political events taking place in the west but also the various ideologies shaping the Western society and reacted to them as a Muslim intellectual. One of such reactions was with regard to socialism. In 1881, Afghani condemned socialism alongwith communism and nihilism as ideologies destructive to human society.[173] However, he later modified his assessment of socialism partially. This is evident in his views expressed on this subject[174] during his stay in Istanbul (1892–97), in response to a question put to him by a Turkish man-of-letters whom Afghani held in high respect. The questioner stated that "the best thing in the European renaissance is socialism—a movement aiming to restore to the working people the rights which have been denied to them. Now if Islam and Muslim shaykhs will go on resisting socialism, it will do irreparable damage which we in wisdom must seek to present." In his reply, Afghani dwelt on the basic weaknesses of socialism and the merits of Islamic socialism. By socialism Afghani understood sharing (*ishtirāk*) by the poor in the wealth and comforts of the rich. His main contention is that the western socialism is a product of the revolt of the poor (*mustaḍ'ifīn*) against their suppression by the well-to-do. Islamic socialism, on the other hand, is inherent in the Arab culture and Islamic teachings. Analysing western socialism, he says that it "owes its being solely to the vindictive feelings against unjust rulers and unjust laws and the jealousy on the part of the workers (*'ummāl*) of those who have grown rich from their labour and toil. These, moreover, accumulated fortunes which are used by them foolishly, extravagantly and wastefully before the very eyes of those who produced it all and got it out, as it were, from the very ground. In short, the diverse needs of civilised life are all of them supplied by the labourers."[175] Again, the exploitation by the rich and reaction of the exploited, both exhibited lack of moderation. "The rich in the West have grossly trifled with the rights of the workers and that of the poor, and these in turn have gone too far in their defiance of those who have robbed them of their rights, who only seem to care for position and prestige."[176] Here, religion becomes relevant. "Socialism, with no religious foundation, and with no authority to restrain and work for the general good, can only introduce chaos and must eventually suffer a reverse."[177]

Socialism, in the Islamic context, is not a consequence of any social or economic development, but is inherent in Islamic teachings. It is "a part and parcel of the religion of Islam; it is also closely related to the character of its peoples from the time when they were nomad peoples."[178] Afghani refers to the cultural trait of the pagan Arabs of their rich helping the poor of their tribe. Citing the example of Ḥātim of Taiy and Ṭalḥa of Talhas who used to offer whatever they had to meet the needs of the needy,

Afghani draws attention to the fact that the help was asked by and offered to the needy not out of any obligation as such, but it was a feature of the Arab culture itself. "This may be taken as an example of the kind of socialism they had before Islam. And while assets remained private property, they were well used and shared; that was what made socialism acceptable and admirable. There was no selfishness and no arrogance *vis-a-vis* the poorer people just because one had a noble horse, or delicacies to be enjoyed in company, or a fine house to live in, while the one who created all the riches, the poor labourer, occupied a poor shack with no leg room and having his children outside exposed to the freezing cold and the scorching heat with not enough bread to still his hunger or clothes to cover his nakedness.

"This is what the wealthy are like at the present day and this is what makes the working classes resort to socialism; they are vindictive. Their exaggerated claims are met with complete unconcern and even their most elementary rights are treated with indifference. This must work up to a grave situation in the West, which will not leave the East unaffected."[179]

Afghani, further strengthens his contention of socialism being rooted in Islam by quoting the Qur'an. Firstly, in its very, first chapter the Qur'an highlights the principle of human equality through God's being 'the Lord of the Worlds' (*Rabb al-'Ālamīn*), that is, He is the only God of all human beings, Muslims being a part of all other created beings in the world. Secondly, Qur'an at several places has instructed for sharing (*ishtirāk*) of all the wealth obtained in a war by all. The Qur'an commands that the warriors and the conquerers should protect the rights of the weak who do not participate in *jihād* and should have a share of the spoils of the war.[180] Besides the shares to Allah and the Prophet, the third share must go to *Dhawi'l Qurba* (the relatives), that is, the weak (*al-mustaḍ 'ifīn*) who, for some reason or other, "did not take part in the fighting nor helped to get the loot, but must not on that account be deprived of a share (of the spoil) which was obtained by the strong who risked their lives in the attempt."[181] Afghani holds that this was based "on the wisdom of sharing, or *ishtirāk* as was the practice, to the mutual satisfaction of those who did the fighting and those who did not. After God and the Prophet, priority was given to those related to the warriors according to their affinity to those who looked after their children in their absence. Next come those who were not so related, here named 'orphans'. The sharing is then made to include the poor, *al-masākīn*; the sharing was made to go still further so as to include the wayfarer. This then was a from of socialism of which there is none better or more inclusive". Again, the Qur'an "censures those who accumulate riches and commends those who unselfishly support and feed the poor, although they may go short themselves."[182]

Afghani then cites the examples of the personalities who set examples of 'socialist' living according to Islam, particularly, the Prophet and the early caliphs Abū Bakr and 'Umar. The first such instance was the fraternity established by the Prophet among the *Muhājirīn* (the immigrants) and the *Ansārs* (the helpers) in Madinah. It was "a noble piece of work and an unmistakable example as to how sharing was accepted to the letter. This arrangement enabled the emigrant Muslim without compromising his religion contentedly to leave his country and domicile, his kith and kin, his property and possessions, happy to reach Medina in safety. The helper on his part, remaining where he was with his folk, his home and possessions, was content to share everything with his emigrant brother." This selflessness and refinement, Afghani emphasizes, could be generated only by religion.[183]

Islam, he further argues, treats a social system defective if there is a vast gulf between the rich and the poor. Wealth in quantity and quality is something to be shared with the poor and not to be accumulated by a few to the envy of others. Islamic teachings suggest ways and means to bridge the gulf between the rich and the poor. *Zakāt* is one of them which is levied on one's capital. The other measures include distribution of one fifth of the war booty and charity among the needy.[184] With regard to the Islamic prohibition of usury (*ribā*), Afghani states: "Where the situation demanded it, the Imam could allow a reasonable interest, but this should not overburden the debtor nor would it at any time exceed the (original) capital. The Qur'an thus differentiated (between such creditors and) fraudulent usurers who taking religion as a cloak and pretending to eschew usury (resorted to the legal fiction) of selling some commodity at three times its value to the hard pressed buyer, the difference in price being nothing else than the usury (for the loan). This is how they deceive themselves, claiming that they did not transgress the law which forbade usury."[185]

Afghani compares the pre-Islamic and Islamic society with reference to the distortions produced by wealth or the wealthy in a social system.[186] In the pre-Islamic, *Jāhilīya*, period the difference between the very rich and the poor in terms of material amenities was not much and therefore there were no feelings of jealousy or hatred towards the rich among the poor people. During the early period of Islam, the caliphs led a life of austerity as practised by the Prophet in spite of the flow of wealth through war-booty. Under Abū Bakr's caliphate the Arab society maintained this life-style. However, during the period of the second Caliph 'Umar, in the wake of accumulation of wealth pouring in from various parts of the empire, all the vices of affluence appeared among the high state-officials. Governors including Mu'āwiya (Iraq) or 'Amr ibn al-'Āṣ (Egypt), commanders and other high officials adopted all manners of luxurious living. 'Umar, observing in this trend a threat to the whole social structure, started taking stringent measures to check it. He admonished them and confiscated half the properties of the governors. "This was a lesson which all Muslims could appreciate that ruler and ruled alike were to put away greed, selfishness and conceit." 'Umar himself led a very austere life.

During the period of the third Caliph, 'Uṭhmān, the spiritual condition (*ḥālāt al-rūḥīya*) of the Muslim community changed. The earlier simplicity gave way to luxurious living. This appeared mainly among the Caliph's kith and kin, princes and the high officials. The society was divided into various classes: the princes, nobles and the rich, on the one hand, and, on the other, the labouring classes and the sons of the warriors who had earlier defended Islam and established Muslim state. The latter, not being a part of the government and the nobility, could not lead a prosperous life. Along with the increase of luxurious living among the nobles and government officials and the fief-holders, vices like pride and arrogance also appeared. This situation, according to Afghani's analysis, gave rise to class conflict and the labouring classes produced "a class of intelligent poor who seeing the injustice of it all began to ask for their rights and they knew them from scripture and the exemplary lives of the first two caliphs." Afghani cites the example of Abū Dhar Ghifāri, a Companion of the Prophet, as the most outspoken critic of the rich. Realising the damage inherent in this development, he approached Mu'āwiya and "spoke to him of the need for turning back to live the life of the pious ancestors, to curb opulence and to put a stop to those things which make for envy and to eradicate them from the Muslim governing classes. He exhorted him at great length and recounted the potential danger from the impoverished but intelligent labouring classes. They themselves, enduring hardships and deprivations, were living among people who were enjoying a life of ease despite the fact that neither they nor their fathers did anything for Islam, nor were they superior in any way by reason of character, by services rendered or by physical powers or learning, to give them the right to the luxuries they were enjoying, apart from the fact that they were connected with army leaders and government officials."

Mu'āwiya replied that he could do nothing in this regard except urging peoples to give more alms; "he could but counsel and softly exhort to abstain from what might excite envy, but could do nothing more." Abū Dhar left in disgust and exhorted those suffering under hardships "to rise and demand what was their due and was taken from them by people without any legal sanction with no precedent to go on. This resulted in a commotion and Mu'āwiah and his partisans feared the dire consequences that might follow." Mu'āwiah referred this matter to the Caliph 'Uthmān who called Abū Dhar. Abū Dhar repeated to the Caliph the saying of the Prophet that when the built up areas in Madinah, soaring and spreading should extend to mount Sal'a one should emigrate : "The buildings put up by you and Mu'āwiah, your kinsman, have reached towering heights. I therefore bid you farewell, leaving you your work and that of your agent." Afghani comments that what Abū Dhar did was to advise the Caliph and his officials "to protect the rights of Muslims and thus forestall the formation of a socialist faction motivated by feelings of revenge, and urged them to do as the scriptures say and implement it in the manner of Abū Bakr and 'Umar."

Afghani sums up his analysis by asserting that the true, reasonable and beneficial socialism is only the Islamic socialism as practised by the two Caliphs, Abū Bakr and 'Umar. Any other type of socialism may be only 'a catchword' and 'must end up in bloodshed, the massacre of the innocents and a devastation which will benefit no one.'[187]

The above description shows that Afghani's understanding of socialism was confined to the basic socialistic concept of sharing (*ishtirāk*) by the weak in the wealth of the rich. He does not appear to be aware of socialism being a system of life and state. For him, socialism was a negative movement, initiated by the poor out of jealousy and vindictiveness against the rich. Whereas, Islamic socialism, based on a firm religious concern for the uplift of the poor and weak sections of the people, functions as a policy of the Islamic state. Obviously, Afghani's understanding of socialism, in the early stage of the development of this concept, was only partially valid in as much as he considered it as a product of the reaction of the down-trodden, while its being a full-fledged economic and social system was either not appreciated or rejected by him. In any case, Afghani's description of socialism as rooted in Arab culture and Islam, made in as early a period as the last decade of 19th century, deserves attention as being the first attempt at defining Islamic socialism (*ishtirākīyat al-Islām*) in the modern history of Muslim thought.[188]

References

1. Nikki R. Keddie holds that Afghani was born in Asadābād, Iran, without drawing any conclusion about his being a *Shi'a*. *Biography*, Chapter 2.

2. *Risālah*, p. 9; See also SH, p. 101; *Sharh*, p. 83; *Āthār*, p. 123. His being *Sunni* was a well known fact. When Afghani was invited by Nāṣiruddīn Shāh to visit Persia and was offered the post of Prime Minister and he accepted the invitation, he was warned by his friend Shaikh 'Abdul Qādir al-Maghribi to be on his guard. "How could he invite you to fill such a position, seeing that you are notorious for your efforts to strengthen the Sunni faith ?" To this the Sayyid replied: "Mere fancy and folly on his part." E.G. Browne, *The Persian Revolution* (Cambridge, 1910), p. 10; 'Abdul Qādir al-Maghribi, *Jamāl al-Dīn al-Afghāni* (Egypt, 1947), p. 80

3. W. S. Blunt, *India under Ripon* (London, 1900), p. 4. E.G. Browne, op. cit., p. 402. For a similar view, see *Risālah*, p. 10

4. *Documents*, pp. 11-15. For the influence of Shaikhi school, *Cf. Biography*, p. 19 ff.

5. *Documents*, p. 14, doc. 9, pl. 7, photo, 18; tr. *Biography*, p. 38
6. *Sharh*, pp. 107-8
7. *Risālah*, p. 9; *Sharh*, p. 85
8. Azhar Amratsari, *Paighām-i-Ḥaq* (Lahore, Jan.-Feb., 1947), p. 82; See also Furşat al-Dawla Shīrāzi, *Dīwān-i-Furṣat* (Tehran, 1338 Solar), p. 24
9. *Paighām-i-Ḥaq*, p. 76
10. *Sharh*, pp. 87-89
11. *Paighām-i-Haq*, p. 82
12. ibid.
13. *Sharh*, ibid.
14. ibid., pp. 89-90. According to an account, he gave lectures on astronomy on the basis of a book written in English. *Dīwān-i-Furṣat*, p. 20
15. *Sharh*, ibid.
16. *Cf.* pp. 56 below ff.
17. For instance, while explaining the outdated astronomical researches of the early Muslim scholars, Afghani advised one of his disciples, Mirza Muhammad 'Ali Khān Sadid Al-Salṭanah, to study the works of modern astronomers, who had refuted all the ancient notions of astronomy and proved the modern theories by rational arguments. *Dīwān-i-Furṣat*, pp. 18-20
18. M, p. 95
19. *Zu'amā*, p. 114
20. *Al-Manār*, viii, pp. 399-400
21. SH, p. 102
22. *Cf.* p. 57 below ff.
23. *'Urwah*, i, p. 88
24. ibid., pp. 88-89
25. ibid., p. 89
26. *Cf.* Chap. III, p. 77 below ff.
27. ibid.
28. H, pp. 70-71
29. H, pp. 21-34; *Cf.* Chap. III, p. 77 ff.
30. *Al-'Urwah al-Wuthqā* (Cairo, 1957), p. 11
31. ibid.
32. H, pp. 74-83
33. ibid., p. 12
34. ibid., pp. 75-76
35. ibid., pp. 75-76
36. ibid., pp. 76-79
37. Francois Guizot (1787-1874), the French statesman and historian, wrote this brilliant work, in six volumes, in 1829-32. (Eng. tr. by William Hazlitt, 3 Vols., 1846). It is incomplete and covers principally the civilization of France upto the 14th century
38. H, p. 70
39. Maghribi, op. cit., pp. 95-96
40. H, pp. 79-82
41. *Khāṭirāt* (Arabic), pp. 137-39. *Khāṭirāt* (Persian), pp. 76-78

42. ibid.
43. *Khāṭirāt* (Arabic), pp. 141-42
44. M, p. 165
45. Shaikh Muḥammad Mahallāti, *Guftār i Khush-i-Yār Quli* (Tehran, 1327 A.H.), p. 59
46. M, p. 139
47. *Sharh*, pp. 97-8
48. Mahallāti, op. cit., pp. 59-60
49. M, pp. 139-140
50. Murtaḍa Mudarrisi Chahārdihi, *Zindagāni wa Falsafa-i Ijtimā'i wa Siyāsi-i Sayyid Jamāl al-Dīn* (Tehran, 1334 A.H.), p. 123
51. Article in *Pall Mall Gazette*, Dec. 30, 1891, quoted, *Biography*, pp. 361-62
52. ibid.
53. Maghribi, op. cit., pp. 57-59
54. Vol. I, published in 1880; Vol. II, 1882; Vol. III, 1885; Vol. IV, 1888; Vol. V, 1892; Vol. VI, 1895. Afghani's criticism is based on the first two volumes.
55. M, pp. 100-101
56. *Khāṭirāt* (Arabic), pp. 99-100
57. ibid., pp. 100-1
58. ibid., pp. 102-3
59. ibid., pp. 100-1
60. ibid., pp. 103-4
61. See the following discussion on '*Aqīdah*
62. '*Urwah*, pp. 161-2
63. ibid., p. 216
64. M, p. 104
65. ibid., pp. 102-4
66. M, pp. 102-104
67. Mahallāti, op. cit., p. 59
68. '*Urwah*, i, pp. 161-62
69. *Cf.* pp. 173 above ff.
70. SH, p. 102
71. ibid., p. 101
72. *Sharh*, p. 89
73. *Zu'amā*, p. 113
74. ibid. See also SH, p. 102. He does not appear to have a very high opinion of the existing *fiqh* literature which he finds full of contradictions, *cf.* Anwar al-Jundi, *al-Sharq fi Fajr al-Yaqzam* (Cairo, 1969), pp. 30-33, quoted in *Biography*, p. 304
75. *Sharh*, p. 109
76. *Zu'amā*, p. 113, *Khāṭirāt* (Arabic), pp. 111-12
77. ibid.
78. ibid.
79. *Paighām-i-Ḥaq*, p. 71
80. '*Urwah*, i, pp. 161-74
81. ibid., pp. 163-64

82. ibid., p. 164
83. ibid.
84. ibid., p. 165
85. ibid.
86. ibid.
87. W. Montgomery Watt, *Free Will and Predestination in Early Islam* (London, 1948), p. 142
88. ibid., p. 155
89. '*Urwah*, i, p. 167
90. ibid., p. 168
91. ibid., pp. 168-69
92. ibid., pp. 170-71
93. ibid., pp. 171-72
94. Salim Effendi, *al-Ukhuwwa fi'l Islām*, op. cit., *Paighām-i-Ḥaq*, pp. 48-49
95. 'Aqil 'Alavi, *Kawākib al-Sharq*, cit., ibid., p. 74
96. ibid., p. 41
97. Salim Effendi, op. cit., p. 49
98. '*Urwah* (1957 edition), p. 10
99. Salim Effendi, op. cit., p. 51
100. SH, pp. 124-25; *Sharh* p. 112
101. '*Urwah* (1957 edition), p. 10
102. '*Urwah*, (1957 edition), ii, p. 10
103. Haidar Bamat, cit., '*Urwah* (1957 edition), p. 25
104. Salīm Effendi, op. cit., pp. 59-60
105. *Khāṭirāt* (Persian), pp. 84-85; *Khāṭirāt* (Arabic), pp. 52-53
106. ibid.
107. ibid., p. 84
108. ibid., p. 87
109. *Dīwān-i Furṣat*, p. 25
110. ibid., pp. 26-27
111. ibid., pp. 23-24
112. ibid., p. 25
113. TBI, p. 62
114. Art. "al-Ḥukūma al-Istibdādiya," *Miṣr*, ii, no. 33, 1897, tr. L.M. Kenny, "al-Afghani on Types of Despotic Government", *Journal of the American Oriental Society*, 86, 1, 1960, pp. 19-27
115. ibid.
116. '*Urwah* (1957 edition), p. 10
117. ibid.
118. ibid.
119. ibid., p. 11
120. Salīm Effendi, op. cit., p. 50
121. ibid., pp. 49-50
122. Maḥmūd Qāsim, *Jamāl al-Din al-Afghāni, Ḥayātuhū wa Falsafatuhū* (Cairo, n.d.), p. 42; Muḥammad Pāshā Makhzūmi, cit., *al-'Urwah* (1957 edition), Introduction.
123. Salīm Effendi, op. cit., p. 50

124. ibid., p. 51

125. ibid., p. 63. It should be noted that the Young Turks movement in the form of the Committee of Union and Progress (1889-1897) held similar views regarding the political setup in Turkey. *Cf.* E. E. Ramsaur, *Young Turks, Prelude to the Revolution of 1908* (New Jersey, 1957), p. 43

126. *'Urwah*, i, p. 218

127. *'Urwah*, ii, pp. 9-10

128. ibid., i p. 113

129. *'Urwah* (1958 edition), pp. 382-87

130. *'Urwah* (1957 edition), p. 11

131. Letter of Afghani to a high dignitary of the Ottoman Government, *Documents*, photos 26-27. *Cf. Biography*, pp. 131-38, for a detailed analysis of the letter.

132. ibid.

133. Art. "Asbāb al-Ḥarb bi Miṣr," (Reasons for War with Egypt), *al-Manār*, Cairo, xxv, pp. 756-60, reprinted from the *Bee/an-Naḥla*, London, V. 3. As suggested by Keddie, this was probably Afghani's first reference to Pan-Islamism. *Biography*, p. 184

134. ibid. It is to be noted here that Afghani was aware of the distinction between *'aṣabīyah* and *ta'aṣṣub* *Ta'aṣṣub*, according to him, is the application of *'aṣabīyah* for the preservation and defence of one's own community, *'Urwah* (1958 edition), pp. 382-87. However, it has been misused by the Muslims in a negative sense (fanaticism) damaging their own interests. Afghani's speech in 1879, *Miṣr*, May 24, 1879, quoted, *Biography*, pp. 108-9

135. Open letter to *al-Baṣīr*, Paris, Feb. 8, April 26, 1883, quoted, op.cit., p. 185

136. *'Urwah*, i, pp. 221-22; *Sharh*, p. 109

137. ibid.

138. *Paighām-e-Ḥaq*, p. 63

139. *'Urwah* (1957 edition), p. 29

140. Art. "Al-Ḥakīm 'al-Sharq," *Miṣr*, 11, No. 47, May 24, 1879, tr. *Biography*, pp. 108-10

141. ibid.

142. M, pp. 88-89

143. *Khāṭirāt* (Arabic), pp. 85-86

144. ibid.

145. ibid. pp. 87-88

146. *'Urwah*, i, pp. 119-20

147. W. S. Blunt, *Gordan at Khartoum* (London, 1911), p. 492. Afghani states that he suggested to Sharif al-Husain to claim the Caliphate, but the latter pointed out that it was not possible to do so without armed support. ibid.

148. W. S. Blunt, op. cit., pp. 467-68

149. ibid., p. 500

150. ibid., p. 358

151. ibid.

152. *'Urwah*, ii, pp. 172-75

153. ibid., p. 124

154. ibid.
155. ibid., p. 128
156. TBI, p. 89; E. G. Browne, op. cit., p. 82. He favoured the Sultan for the Caliphate reluctantly and mostly because of the respect he enjoyed among the Muslims.
157. *Sharh*, pp. 57-58. For other contemporary accounts of his Pan-Islamic activities, see, *Biography*, pp. 373 ff.
158. *Sharh*, pp. 57-58
159. E. G. Browne, op. cit., pp. 83-84; TBI, pp. 89-90; *Sharh*, p. 59; *Biography*, pp. 380 ff.
160. *Biography*, pp. 377-81 ff.
161. ibid.
162. *Cf.* pp. 19 above ff.
163. *Paighām-e-Ḥaq*, pp. 39-40
164. ibid., pp. 40-41
165. ibid., p. 40
166. ibid., p. 41
167. ibid., pp. 42-43
168. ibid., p. 43. See also *Revue Du Monde Mussulman*, March, 1913, art., "Panislamisme et Panturquisme," p. 194
169. '*Urwah*, i, pp. 89-95
170. Mathew, v, 39
171. ibid., p. 94
172. 'Aqil 'Alavi, cit., *Paighām-e-Ḥaq*, p. 75
173. *Cf.* Chap. IV, pp. 93ff. infra
174. *Khāṭirāt* (Arabic), pp. 118-30. Eng. tr. Sami A. Hanna, "Al-Afghani : A Pioneer of Islamic Socialism," *Muslimt World*, Vol. LVII, No. 1, January 1967.
175. *Khāṭirāt*, p. 120
176. ibid.
177. ibid.
178. ibid.
179. ibid., p. 121
180. ibid., p. 122
181. ibid.
182. ibid.
183. ibid., p. 123
184. ibid.
185. ibid., pp. 123-24. Afghani quotes the following Qur'anic verses : "Those who swallow usury cannot rise up save as he ariseth whom the devil hath prostrated by (his) touch. That is because they say : 'Trade is just like usury'; whereas Allah permitteth trading and forbiddeth usury. He unto whom an admonition from his Lord cometh, and (he) refraineth (in obedience thereto), he shall keep (the profits of) that which is past, and his affair (henceforth) is with Allah. As for him who returneth (to usury)—such are rightful owners of the Fire. They will abide therein." (2 : 275)

"Allah hath blighted usury and made almsgiving fruitful. Allah loveth not the impious and guilty." (2 : 276)

"O ye who believe! Devour not usury, doubling and quadrupling the (sum lent). Observe your duty to Allah, that ye may be successful." (3 : 130)

"If ye publish your almsgiving, it is well, but if ye hide it and give it to the poor, it will be better for you, and will atone for some of your ill-deeds. Allah is informed of what ye do." (2 : 271)

"The alms are only for the poor and the needy, and those who collect them, and those whose hearts are to be reconciled, and to free the captives and the debtors, and for the cause of Allah, and (for) the wayfarers; a duty imposed by Allah. Allah is Knower, Wise". (9 : 60)

"Lo! good deeds annul ill deeds. This is a reminder for the mindful." (11 : 114)

186. ibid., pp. 124-29

187. ibid., p. 129

188. *Hanna*, op. cit., p. 24

TWO

INDIVIDUAL AND SOCIETY

INDIVIDUAL

The purpose of this chapter is to investigate Afghani's views on the individual and society and their mutual relation. It also includes a study of the rights and responsibilities of the individual towards society and the nature of education preparing him for the service of society. It would be noticed that the method which he adopts to tackle these issues is more empirical than idealistic. Even when he offers a purely theoretical treatment he endeavours to refrain from philosophical analysis. His chief emphasis is upon those human sentiments, dispositions, and intellectual aptitudes which form the basis of social or national structure and are instrumental in the realization of national aims.

As we shall see in the study of Afghani's ethical ideas he places social values above everything else while judging individual conduct. Individual, for Afghani, is the foundation stone upon which the whole structure of society rests. Man is not superior to other animals as far as the basic instincts are concerned; it is only the urge for a nobler and civilised life which gives shape to his social personality.[1] Explaining the position of the individual in society he gives primary importance to human emotions which, being natural, play an essential role in deciding the direction of human conduct. Such a psychological study shows that man is a born artisan (*ṣannā'*). All his comforts and luxuries are his thoughts in material from.[2] Man is not nature but he is everywhere bound to nature. Nature is generous to the man of action and it neglects one who just begs for her generosity. For all his social necessities man needs nature as an artisan requires his instrument.[3] The object around which all individual activities revolve is man's own good. The impetus for human will to develop into action is derived from the purpose which provides the greatest benefit to oneself.[4] The impetus is ever present in all social relations. Afghani realistically points out that even blood ties find strength from one's urge to remain in close contact with those who are indispensable for the fulfilment of one's immediate needs. Thus, the existence of family institutions is directly a result of social necessity.[5] Therefore, such ties operate only so long as the necessities are there. No sooner do they disappear than the binding force of such ties is weakened. It is the same with other ties. Social necessities govern all human relations which by incessent practice, under constant social pressure, are transformed into deep-rooted habits. Once free of such pressure they lose their colour and are reduced to obscure ideas.[6] Whatever their basis, institutions like family, tribe or nation exert great influence on the making of individual personality and outlook. As a psychic being man's thoughts, morals and outlook, whether physical or metaphysical, are to a large extent influenced by his parents and the members of his tribe or community.[7] However, Afghani points out, such influences are less effective upon human mind which is chiefly governed by rational faculties. Man learns more from his teachers and his experiences in life.[8] We shall study later[9] his views on individual conduct, the nature of human emotions and the need of controlling them for the sake of social welfare. As a whole he regards all individuals blessed equally with physical and mental capacity for highest attainments. The faculty of reason is the most powerful and noble means to achieve that aim. While all human instincts should be satisfied fully they must not exceed limits set down by reason. For the maintenance of society and individual livelihood they should function under the guidance of the intellect.[10] All individual struggles revolve round the goal of attaining an honourable life and the rest is a means to reach that end.[11] The nature of this honour (*sharaf*) is such that when achieved by an individual it is shared by all around him, that is, by his family, tribe, community and his country. He struggles for respectable positions by acquiring those noble qualities which help in establishing himself as a trustworthy person in society.[12] While acting for his own benefit he serves society as well. He is conscious of the importance of collective working of a social group. Unity is the basic condition of social progress. However, Afghani states, this desire for unity is not born of abstract thinking. It is produced by a deep insight into the inner meanings of social intercourse.[13] Consequently, the actions of such socially conscious individuals are determined by the maximum benefits which they attempt to provide to society.[14] In view of this fact the individual refrains from pursuing aims other than social welfare. Each individual functions in a society as a part of a big machine. The weekness of any single part, howsoever small, means the breakdown of the whole system.[15] Since the actions of individuals have their effect on society, the strength of the society depends on the unity of the individuals.[16] Again, there are several branches of knowledge which help in the fulfilment of social needs and it is not possible for a single individual to cover all sciences. Therefore, persons working in different fields of knowledge have to co-operate with each other.[17] Having common aims makes individuals realize their responsibilities and obligations regarding common good.[18]

Society

A thorough analysis of society is found in the essay, "*al-sanā'a*" (craftsmanship)[19] where Afghani has discussed the evolution of man from a self-centred individualist to a coordinated social personality. Emphasising the social nature of human beings he remarks that man has not descended from heaven; he is one of the creatures living on earth. The primitive man led a wild life living under trees or taking shelter in the caves. There were no traces of civilization or arts and crafts. He had no education (*tarbiya*) of any kind. He had no idea that the universe was created for human beings. In support of this thesis Afghani cites the wild tribes still residing in the South African forests who are far from civilization notwithstanding their long history. It was the faculty of reason which helped man to take a step forward towards civilization. Afghani explains that God had made man in such a way that his needs could not be fulfilled without struggle. At the same time man had been endowed with the power of thinking and acquiring knowledge. He attained wisdom from actions and reactions. Sometimes his activity was checked by natural obstacles and at times truth was revealed to him by chance happenings. Through this process he entered the era of civilization. He marched forward with the help of arts and crafts towards which he was led by his power of thinking. Arts served him as a substitute for those faculties and organs with which the animals have been provided by nature. For instance weaving is equivalent to the animals' ability of growing hair and man-made weapons to animal claws and nails, etc.

Afghani remarks that human actions are generally performed under the guidance of reason. Reason as against sense (*ḥiss*) moves from universal to particular. God has made it the axis of human betterment. If man confines the use of intellect to his personal requirements it means that he wastes his abilities and degenerates to the level of animals and plants.

Afghani, explaining the need of society, points out that a social organisation is indispensable to mankind in view of the fact that individual requirements are so numerous that it is not possible for an individual to meet them single-handed even during a long span of time. Hence, the need of an organisation where different individuals, in their own ways, could help each other in fulfilling the requirements of all. A man receives the cost of his labour in the form of the results emanating from the works of others.[20]

Afghani describes society in terms of human body. Each organ functions for the maintenance of the whole body so that the benefit received by it from the organs returns again to each of them. If an organ or individual acts in isolation from the organisation it means that he is unconsciously destroying himself. That is why each man should act as a strong member of society and perform actions beneficial to all. Afghani states that individuals not working for society should be discarded, since such men exercise a harmful influence on others.[21] In this connection Afghani condemns people who do not make full use of their talents and give themselves up to *tawakkul*, wrongly interpreted as absolute reliance upon God. He describes it as going against natural laws.[22]

According to the above analysis individual necessities have urged men towards the formation of society. Social organisation has manifested itself in different kinds of units at different stages, such as family, tribe, and community. Each unit has a binding force which gives it the shape it possesses. Afghani calls it the

'Spirit of Life' (*Rūḥ-i-Ḥayāt*). This spirit of life controls each unit and by coordinating its energies pushes it forward towards progress.[23]

First, there is a human being composed of elements having qualities quite different from each other and organs with different shapes performing various actions. Human soul unifies these different elements and organs to function for the maintenance of the whole human body and thus ensures the existence of the individual.

The second unit is that of the family (*waḥdat-i-baitīya*). Its life spirit is close relationship which unites men of different temperaments, aims and ambitions to act for common objective —maintenance of the whole family.

The third unit is that of clan (*waḥdat-i-'ashīra*) which is formed by the coming together of several families. The life-spirit of such a group is described by Afghani as absolute relationship (*qarābat-i-muṭlaqa*). It harmonises the thoughts and actions of the members of all families to support the common cause of that tribe.

The final unit is that of community (*Qaum*) which is composed of several tribes. As may be gathered from his views, the basic elements on the basis of which a group of people may be called a community are unity of language, thought and religion. Language is the broadest basis upon which people following different religions may form a community.[24] However, it is the unity of thought and action without which no kind of grouping can be possible—a point often emphasised by Afghani. He calls this urge for unity as the life-spirit of a community. Among the peoples who possess this spirit all classes will function in full coordination having the same moving force (*quwwah-i-muḥrika*). The individuals may move in different directions but still serve a common purpose. They may proceed in opposite directions as upon a circumference and will inevitably come nearer to each other. By this illustration Afghani seems to emphasise individual freedom of action as well as social responsibilities. Besides, he states that human actions, customs and manners, modes of livelihood, and the pattern of a nation's working depend on rational thoughts, and spiritual qualities of that nation. So, the harmony of action implies harmony in thought and qualities. As it is, base dispositions and false thoughts are outwardly in harmony, but are actually quite opposed to each other. Persons having such thoughts and habits tend to disagree with one another. Therefore, Afghani remarks, there should be certain thoughts and qualities which could maintain balance among the base and the noble thoughts and qualities. Afghani points out that the thought and qualities having a balancing force are only those which create unity and harmony among individuals and aim at the good of the whole. Hence, they are called noble dispositions and sublime thoughts.[25] They are also described as virtues. Virtues are those qualities which, when acquired and nurtured, can produce the required harmony and unity of thought. They develop a sense of social justice in individuals, help them in avoiding conflicts and transform them into one cohesive whole moving by one single will and advancing towards one common goal.[26] Individual interests should give way to the common cause of society. Again, besides observance of moral values, a rational outlook is also a basic condition for the smooth working of society. Harmony in people's actions depends upon moral purity which cannot be achieved without the help of reason. Therefore, for the happiness of a nation both moral and rational pattern of thinking and action are necessary.[27] As such, the main point of emphasis is always the unity of thought and action among the nation-builders, scholars, teachers, jurists, artists, craftsmen, farmers, traders, soldiers, men of letters, etc. Society's material and intellectual life, thus depends upon the smooth functioning of all these classes (*ṭabaqāt*) in complete cooperation. On the other hand, a nation is ruined when the unity of thought weakens affecting the unity of the whole organisation and cooperation among its classes.[28]

Investigating the cause behind the lack of coordination among classes and individuals, Afghani reverts to morality holding that personal ambitions often throw the individuals into a state of constant conflicts and struggle with one another.[29] He agrees that pursuit of pleasure is the soul of human activities. However, the main point is that men do not know what is pleasure and where it lies. All men have their own conceptions of pleasure which they struggle to attain in their own ways. There are people who aspire for wealth, some hope to build palaces and gardens, and others love high offices. In these blind pursuits, greed and selfishness they ignore the comforts and peace of thousands of other people and do not hesitate to deprive the weak and the poor of their livelihood.[30] Afghani remarks that this selfish attitude of seeking one's own comforts at the cost of others is the result of ignorance as to the real meaning of pleasure. He believes that an individual's pleasure and comfort reside in the pleasures and comforts of the whole society. The main trouble, he points out, is that man desires to confine pleasures and comforts absolutely to himself. Afghani asserts that a man who usurps the properties and wealth of others cannot live happily. The mass of people whose rights and comforts are snatched away would not always remain passive. Their hatred would always be a danger to the safety of such usurpers.[31] In his characteristic style, Afghani points out the contradictions of such an unbalanced society by stating: "What comfort is there in a grand palace which is erected in a country full of sufferings ? . . .What happiness is there for those in high posts who have nothing around them but a mass of shabbily dressed poor people ? . . . Of what use is the wealth from which no benefit can be derived by anyone ? How can one take a morsel of food while he is listening to the cries of thousands of hungry wretches all around him ?"[32] Afghani declares that man could attain comfort and pleasure only in a country where each class of society enjoys all things equally.[33]

It should be noted that while denouncing exploitation by the upper classes Afghani has departed from an exclusively theological approach in the judgement of social evils. His insistance upon equal distribution of comforts among all the classes of a society, though expressed rather vaguely, shows that he was inclined to interpret social issues not only from a purely religious standpoint but also in a way which reminds us of the socialistic thinking which was getting firm ground in Europe towards the middle of 19th century. However, it will be wrong to conclude that he subscribed to the theories of socialism or communism which he condemned vehemently as we shall see later.[34] It only shows that he was liberal enough to take into account facts besides religion in his evaluation of society.

Education (*Tarbiya*)

In Afghani's view the purpose of education is to prepare the individual for the service of the nation. Afghani states that education amounts to a struggle with and a resistance to nature (*ṭabī'at*). It does not imply, however, that he advocates the suppression of nature; what he means is that such desires and ambitions should be resisted as may lead a person astray. This point he makes clear by stating that a good education lifts one's nature from imperfection to excellence and from baseness to nobility.[35] It is only through education that man acquires the character of a human being.

Afghani regards the spirit of nationalism (*qaumīyat*) as the chief purpose towards which education should be directed. Nationalism is a state of mind which is produced in the individual by regular schooling. Once this mental attitude is built up, the individual regards the prestige of his nation as his own.[36] Such education helps in the harmonious functioning of different groups and classes which is a primary condition for the progress of society. A nation, thus unified, produces great philosophers, religious scholars, artists, agriculturists, traders, etc. In view of the fact that the interest of the individual is connected with that of society. Afghani holds that the former should be prepared for the service of the latter and that individual aims should not take precedence over social objectives. All loyalties should be to one's own country and people.[37] In brief, Afghani lays down three objectives for education : (a) individuals should be prepared for the noblest deeds and worldly positions; (b) their beliefs should have a rational basis; and (c) they should act for the whole society.

Afghani's educational ideas are also reflected in his discussion on knowledge and sciences. In his conception of knowledge and his views on the origin and development of sciences he does not follow the early Muslim thinkers according to whom no knowledge is possible beyond what is contained in the Qur'an or the teachings of the Prophet. As Ibn Ḥazm says, "Any fact whatsoever which can be proved by reasoning is in the Qur'an or in the words of the Prophet, clearly set out."[38] In course of time, this point of view developed into a prejudice against all rational sciences which seemed to defy religious authority. Such an outlook was adopted only at a comparatively later stage in the history of Islam when the predominant influence of the '*Ulamā* made religion dogmatic and exclusive. For, if it would have benn otherwise how can we explain the encouragement exteəded to the studies of Greek sciences under the Abbasid Caliphs at Baghdad, or at the courts of the Persian rulers, or in Egypt under several Fatimid Caliphs, or in Spain under the Umayyads? The hardening of dogmatic feeling in various schools disapproved the philosophers. It was a common belief of the rigid orthodoxy that all philosophers had no faith in the basic tenets of Islam. The antagonistic outlook adopted by the orthodoxy towards rational and social sciences continued during the subsequent centuries and was more active in the later half of the 19th century when Afghani was criticised by the *'Ulamā* of al-Azhar for teaching philosophy to the students.[39]

In a totally unorthodox manner Afghani studies the issue of the origin and development of sciences. He believes that knowledge progresses in accordance with social needs. He traces the development of all sciences along with the exigencies during different stages of social development. He bases this theory upon the assumption that perfection in livelihood (*ma'īshat*) and betterment of life are the basic objectives of rational and spiritual excellence. It is material prosperity which urges human reason to act. In order to achieve this prosperity man rose from the level of wild life to the heights of civilization and culture.[40] The yearning for perfection in life made men discover different arts and crafts, sciences and industries. He had to know the methods of cultivation, construction of canals, wells, bridges, buildings, etc. For maintaining good health a knowledge of the influence of different climates, chemical compositions of various drugs and their effects upon human physique was acquired. As it was practically difficult for each man to learn all these sciences it became more obligatory for those who had mastered a particular science to cooperate with others so that the needs of all could be fulfilled satisfactorily. Thus, with the increasing needs new sciences came into existence and were developed. Afghani enumerates in this regard nearly all natural, physical and social sciences such as physics, chemistry, botany, zoology, physiology, surgery, geography, mathematics, geometry, algebra, coordinate geometry, archaeology, mineralogy, navigation, sociology, civics, and political science.[41]

After having developed social sciences man turned his attention to the problems of human soul. This was necessary in view of the fact that material prosperity, accompanied by the corruption of morals and abuse of spiritual talents, was disastrous for the well being of society. A coward, greedy, jealous, short-tempered, and miserly person could not be at peace with his environment notwithstanding all material comforts. With the aid of philosophy man was able to distinguish between moral and immoral acts so that he may refrain from the latter and acquire virtues which could help him in attaining spiritual perfection. Thus, for the purification of the soul the art of 'refinement of dispositions (*tahdhīb al-akhlāq*) was developed.[42]

Thereafter, man studied problems like the origin and reality of human life, the foundations of consciousness, nature of perception and its relation with physical sensations, the origin of matter, its attributes and accidents, the elements of the universe and the reactions therein, the production of germs in plants and animals and their evolution through different states to a permanent form, the ethical attitudes of different nations and their legal systems and the phenomenon of the rise and fall of world cultures. All these studies brought forth several new sciences like philosophy, ethics, history, jurisprudence, theology, etc.[43]

Afghani holds that it is knowledge which is responsible for man's success. Even military victories, according to him, were brought about by nations by means of superior knowledge.[44] He supports this view by citing the triumphs of the Chaldeans, Egyptians, Phoenicians, Greeks and Christians who established empires by dint of their mastery over sciences. The political penetration of the English and the French in Afghanistan and Tunisia was in fact the triumph of knowledge over ignorance.[45] "The king of the world is science and without it kingship has never existed, does not exist and will not exist. The Chaldeans, Egyptians, Phoenicians, Greeks and the Europeans of modern age have conquered lands and dominated the world not because of their military power but because of their sciences. The military conquests are not of the French or the English but it is science projecting its magnificence and glory and ignorance has no other way except to admit its inferiority and servitude to science. Thus in reality, kingship has never deserted the house of science. However, this real king has always changed its capital—sometimes it has travelled from the East to the West and sometimes from the West to the East."[46] On the relationship between knowledge and the progress of a nation he says that, "If we ponder over the wealth and prosperity of the world, we would find that it is the result of trade, industry and agriculture. Agriculture is not attainable without the science of crafts, chemistry, biology and geometry; industry cannot be achieved without the sciences of physics, chemistry, geometry and arithmetic, and trade depends on industry and agriculture. Thus all prosperity and wealth are the result of science."[47] At another occasion, addressing the peoples of the East, Afghani says, "O sons of the East, don't you know that the power of the Westerners and their domination over you came about through their advance in learning and education, and your decline in these domains? . . . Make the effort to obtain knowledge and become enlightened with the light of truth so as to recoup glory and obtain true independence."[48] Afghani believes that the ideas and trends of a nation largely reflect the thoughts of its philosophers and *'Ulamā*. The progress of a nation mostly depends upon the potentialities of the *Ulamā* and the strength of their thoughts. If they possess good thoughts, pure souls and refined dispositions they would succeed in creating among the people the qualities of love, spiritual dignity and unity.[49] A person, according to Afghani, deserves to be called an *'ālim* only when he is capable of performing the sacred duty of educating and reforming the national character and leading the nation towards supreme happiness.[50] Muslim *'Ulamā,* Afghani points out, do not come up to this standard. They pay no attention to modern sciences, nor have they any desire to study them. Regarding their prejudiced attitude towards modern sciences, Afghani remarks that the *'Ulamā* have classified knowledge into two groups : Muslim sciences, on the one hand, and European sciences, on the other. They are ignorant of the fact that knowledge cannot be exclusively ascribed to any particular group of people. Knowledge should not be judged by men, but men should be tested by their knowledge. Afghani points out a paradox in the attitude of the Muslims towards sciences by stating that they study Aristotle with great pleasure as if Aristotle was a Muslim thinker while the things attributed to Gallileo, Newton or Keppler are declared as heresy (*kufr*). In fact, the originators of knowledge are proof and argument and not Aristotle or Gallileo.[51] Referring to al-Ghazali's contention in *al-Munqidh min al-Ḍulāl*, Afghani states that whosoever holds that Islam is against learning mathematical arguments, philosophical proofs, and physical theories is an enemy of Islam. By holding his religion as opposed to universal truths he refutes his own religion.[52] Afghani complains that the *'Ulamā* pay no attention even to those science which are in daily use. He expresses surprise at the ignorance of these *'Ulamā* who merely read the works of Mullā Ṣadrā and *Shams-i-Bāzigha* and take pride in calling themselves philosophers. They do not enquire into their real worth. They do not want to know the principles of the wireless, ships, and railways. The most curious thing about them is that they go on reading *Shams-i-Bāzigha* throughout the night by the light of a lamp and not for once think why the lamp starts giving smoke when the chimney is taken off and ceases to do so when it is put back."[53] He compares such *'Ulamā* to a wick having a feeble flame which lightens neither its own surroundings nor gives light to others.[54]

Afghani appeals to the Indian *'Ulamā* to study modern sciences and inventions like electricity, magnetism, steam power, wireless, gramophone, photography, telescope and microscope. He asks the *'Ulamā*: "Is it proper on your part to abandon discussion of these modern sciences simply because they are not mentioned in Ibn Sinā's *Shifā* or *Ḥikmat al-Ishrāq* of Shihāb al-Dīn Maqtūl ? Is it not your duty to serve the new generation by your noble thoughts as your predecessors have done in your case?"[55]

Afghani maintains this unprejudiced outlook on sciences in his discussion on the need of learning philoshophy. Contrary to the orthodox practice of condemning the study of philosophy, he strongly advocates its learning and acquiring a philosophical attitude on life. Among all the branches of knowledge, Afghani believes, philosophy is the most comprehensive and essential for building up the character of a nation.[56] Explaining the reasons for the lack of interest shown by the Muslims for philosophy, he states that the real character of philosophy was obscured by numerous definitions, queer words, strange phraseology, and especially by that mental pleasure which the solutions of logical problems provided. In fact, philosophy is a branch of knowledge which realizes the transition from the narrow animal perception to the wide world of human consciousness, exterminates the darkness of false notions by the radiance of intellect, liberates minds from the shackles of ignorance and stupidity and blesses it with culture, wisdom and enlightenment. In short, human life rests on rational behaviour aiming at human perfection.[57] Philosophy teaches man his duties, explains the needs of science and assigns each science its proper function.[58]

Therefore, learning of philosophy is extremely necessary, especially in order to create in a nation what Afghani describes as the 'Spirit of Philosophy' (*Rūḥ-i-Falsafa*). This spirit produces an intellectual outlook which is competent to make full use of different sciences. Scholars without the spirit of philosophy are useless for a nation. No results would accrue from science if they are not coordinated to each other.[59] Again, it is philosophy which helps man to understand each other, explains human nobility and guides them to their proper destinations. The decay of a nation, Afghani points out, shows itself first in the corruption of the 'spirit of philosophy' after which all its sciences, manners and ways of living are vitiated.[60] Emphasising the importance of this spirit, he remarks that if a nation possessed this outlook it would be forced to learn sciences even though it has none of its own. Citing Islamic history he points out that the early Muslims had no sciences but moved by the philosophical spirit which was created by their religion they learned all that was necessary to deal with natural laws and human duties.[61]

Criticism of Muslim Philosophers

Afghani's emphasis on the learning of philosophy and his admiration of the encouragement extended by the early Muslims to sciences is in sharp contrast to his criticism of Muslim philosophers in general. In his article *Fawā'id-i Falsafa*',[62] Afghani remarks that the works of Muslim philosophers are not original or comprehensive.

The issues discussed in those books do not faithfully conform to the Greek originals, nor have the Muslim writers pointed out the mistakes in them. Instead, they were either concealed or adopted in a way that closed the doors of enquiry upon the thinking people. This blind faith in Greek and Roman philosophers was due to the fact that the Muslim thinkers regarded all of them as peoples of pure intellect, holy talents, and true revelations and believed that the truth and authenticity of their views could not be questioned.

Therefore, Muslim writers accepted the arguments of the Greek philosophers in the same way as people follow the opinions of their leaders. For instance, Ibn Sīnā was not courageous enough to refute the views of his teacher Aristotle on the problem of *Nufūs-i-Falakīya* (celestial souls) but merely contented himself by casually expressing his disagreement. Mullā Ṣadrā was so much overawed by the Greeks as to feel convinced that atheism or heresy could not be expected from them. He actually supported the views of Democritus, Empedocles and Epicurius and tried to explain and give lame excuses in favour of their opinions which totally refuted God's existence. Shihāb al-Dīn Maqtūl extended the sphere of *taqlīd* by accepting the utterances of Zoroaster without logical and rational arguments and thus revived the theory of dualism.

This blind faith, Afghani remarks, was probably due to their presupposition that the views of the Greek and Roman philosophers were exclusively original. They overlooked the fact that like all other sciences philosophy had also achieved its present form by going through the process of coordination and harmonization of different thoughts and ideas. Afghani holds that the philosophical sciences, in fact, originated in India and then travelled through Babylonia and Egypt to Greece and Rome acquiring a different form at each stage. What the Greek and Roman philosophers could claim as their own contribution are not more than a few observations and axioms. Since they did not mention the sources of their thoughts the Muslim thinkers treated all Greek and Roman philosophical ideas as original and did not submit them to a critical scrutiny.

Further, according to Afghani, the discussion in the books of Muslim scholars is very much confused and mixed up. Issues concerning physics have not been discussed satisfactorily. Among them, Afghani mentions the nature of matter, form, attributes, extension, void, existence, time and space, the four elements, universe, thunder, lightening, windstorms, earthquakes, plants and animals, the beginning of human life on earth, stars, planets, sun, moon, body, mind, sense, perception, soul, God, causation, creation and purpose of creation, etc. All these subjects which needed exhaustive discussion were lost in confused argumentation.

Describing the works of the early Muslim philosophers as incomplete and defective, Afghani urges upon the *'Ulamā* to put all these useless books aside and acquire a rational outlook, learn modern sciences and direct their wisdom to the reformation and uplift of the Muslims.[63]

Language

Among the basic features underlying the unity of human groups Afghani singles out language as the most prominent unifying factor. There are two major forces which give shape to such unities. They are language and religion.[64] Language unifies people belonging to different groups having different aims, inculcates in them the spirit of nationalism in order to weld divergent social groups into a single cohesive nation pursuing a common goal.[65] The bond of language is more effective and lasting than that of religion; for, a nation changes its religion more than once in, say, a thousand years while its language remains the same. Regarding the range of influence, this 'linguistic unity' has an important advantage over religion. While a religion is confined only to its followers, language may include in its sphere of influence believers in various religions. Hence a Greek Christian is justified in being proud of Plato, Aristotle and Socrates on the ground of common language, while an Indian Christian could claim no such right over Newton or Galileo on relgious grounds.[66] Afghani holds that a national language must be rich with vocabulary fulfilling the needs of different professional classes. As discussed above, a nation is constituted of different classes. For the existence and functioning of these classes the national language should include all the words and terms which are used in the arts and crafts and all the professions. Therefore, the first duty of those who have an insight into the different factors of nationalism is to extend the scope of the national language. It is incumbent upon them to use words, according to the needs of different arts and crafts, in different contexts, keeping in mind their real meanings. Sometimes they should combine two or three words to convey certain meaning. Afghani suggests that words could be borrowed from those languages which closely resemble the national language. In case there is no other alternative, help may be taken according to necessity even from foreign languages.[67] Such borrowed vocabulary should be absorbed in a way that it should not appear alien. If this is done it would inevitably result in establishing the arts and crafts and all the professions on firm foundations. Afghani emphasises that education, sciences, arts and crafts followed by all the classes of a nation should be in the national language in order to build up the character of a nation and to provide happiness and blessings of nationalism to all. He elaborates this statement by pointing out that if the sciences, arts and crafts are in the national language their foundation in a nation would be firm and they would remain intact for a long time. The succeeding generations could derive benefit from the works of their predecessors, enliven their nation and gain fresh honours. On the contrary, if their sciences and arts are in some foreign language there is every possibility of their being extinct in a short time.[68] Afghani supports this argument by referring to Greek history. The Greeks are still benefiting from the books of their ancestors for the simple reason that they are preserved in their own language. Whereas, the Persians could make no use of those sciences although under the reign of the Parthians, for three hundred years, all their sciences and literature were in the Greek language.[69] Further, if the sciences are in the national language they are easily accessible for the people to learn and are more deeply absorbed by them. Besides, a national language makes it possible for each professional class to attain some knowledge of the sciences used in other professions—a thing necessary in order to achieve perfection in all professions. Afghani emphasises that all modern sciences should be translated in the national language. One should not be proud of having piles of books written in the foreign languages and none in his own. Afghani summarises his arguments in the statement that a nation could be proud only of its honour which could not be achieved except by sciences and literature; sciences and literature could be a matter of honour for a nation when they are popular among the people and this is not possible unless they are in the national language.[70]

Educational Reforms

Besides the theoretical aspect of education and language, the issue of educational reforms in the Muslim countries has also invited penetrating criticism of Afghani. He states that the utility of modern sciences and the urgency to popularize them among the Muslims is indisputable. However, no real advantage from modern sciences can be drawn unless they are used properly according to the actual needs of the nation and by keeping up its integrity. He concedes that there is nothing wrong in the argument that one of the chief causes of the backwardness of the Muslims is that they lack modern sciences and, therefore, there should be an all out effort to popularize these sciences by setting up schools all over the Muslim countries on the pattern of European institutions.[71] Afghani accepts this theory in principle but he is not sure of its being practicable. He points out that this task, great as it is, cannot be accomplished unless it is supported, first by a sovereign political power and, secondly, by sound finance. The Muslims, however, lack both these provisions.[72] Besides, educational reforms need time and peace which are not at their disposal in face of the political designs of the foreign powers who are bent upon taking full advantage of the weaknesses of the Muslims. Therefore, Afghani remarks, those who argue that by incessant struggle we would gradually succeed in achieving that goal are miscalculating the trends of the prevailing conditions. If they at all succeeded in educating a few individuals on the modern pattern the nation would gain no real benefit from them. A few educated persons could not reduce the deep rooted grievances of a nation nor their knowledge would transform the whole national outlook and prepare them for rapid advances in the field of modern knowledge. The Muslims, Afghani points out, have no idea of the origin, development, advantages, and objects of modern sciences and they are not intellectually prepared to appreciate the real values of modern knowledge.[73] Such persons would pass on the sciences to other people in exactly the same manner and form as they have learnt them, without taking into account the prevailing thoughts, trends, and manners of their people according to which the education should be adjusted. It is more probable that they would confuse the major problems with the minor ones and, thus, produce wrong results. Afghani expected no real advantage from the establishment of modern schools, since the ideas inherent in such education were the product of European society and did not suit the conditions of Muslim countries. He describes the persons educated on the modern pattern not as the masters of modern sciences but simply as imitators who have no idea of national needs and objectives. The supporters of modern education are like a mother who, out of love, feeds her baby with delicious meat. Naturally it would prove harmful for the baby who is unable to digest anything other than milk. Such people may act in good faith but the consequences may prove harmful to the nation. They unintentionally become a cause of disintegration among the people and invite the foreigners to intervene in the internal affairs in the name of friendship and help. The unpatriotic outlook of such people who describe themselves as the upholders of freedom, nationalism and patriotism is apparent from the manner of their living. They eat, drink, dress, and live in their homes in Western style. All the articles of their daily use are imported from the Western countries.[74] Thus, in exchange of the wealth of their country they obtain those articles which are of cheap quality. By doing so they have destroyed their own industries and deprived their craftsmen and labourers of their bread. For, those artisans and craftsmen could not afford to run their factories with modern equipment, nor do they have enough capital to finance such projects. Afghani remarks that this situation was the result of the fact that modern sciences were carried to the Muslim countries without having prepared the intellectual foundations among the Muslim people. People who fall a prey to the Western mode of living and forsake their own customs and manners are described by Afghani as enemies of the country. Their reason is overpowered by the love of foreign elements, who use them as tools to carry out their own designs. Criticising the governments of Egypt and Turkey which set up modern schools and sent educational delegations to Europe, he stated that such attempts yielded no result. He asks what benefit the Turks and the Egyptians have drawn from their modern institutions. They have proved a total failure as far as political, economic and social objectives are concerned. These countries are as poor as they were before. They have not become powerful enough to defend themselves against their foes.[75] Another reason of the failure of such attempts in the educational field is that the schools opened in Egypt and Turkey have no provision for the teaching of philosophical sciences. Afghani remarks that since there did not exist a philosophical spirit in their outlook, the Muslims could not gain any benefit from modern sciences. They were obliged to send their youths to Europe for education and invite the European teachers to teach in their schools.[76] The progress of the Muslims, according to him, is possible only if the reform is based on religion. The West and the means of its progress should not become mere objects of imitation and if they become so it would degenerate into submission to the West. He appears to suggest that Islam as a dominating faith must take advantage of the successful experience of the West and use it for its own strength.[77]

Afghani was deeply grieved at the poor educational standards of the Muslims. He says that they do not possess sufficient knowledge of the subjects they are taught. For instance, the object of Arabic grammar is to learn reading, speaking and writing of Arabic language. However, the Muslims have made grammar their object of study and spent years and years in useless philosophical discussions over the subject, whereas after having learnt grammar they are not competent even to understand, speak or write Arabic.[78]

Regarding women's status, Afghani advocated for their educational and social uplift. In a lecture delivered in 1879 in Egypt he said : "I am warning you, gentlemen, against thinking that you will attain the qualities of civilization, acquire knowledge and advance toward progress and happinees. . .if knowledge among you is confined to men; I am warning you that you should not ignore that it is impossible for us to emerge from stupidity, from the prison of humiliation and distress, and from the depths of weakness and ignominy as long as women are deprived of rights and ignorant of their duties, for they are the mothers from whom will come elementary education and primary morality. No doubt the first thing carved on the tablet of a man's mind is the strongest and hardest to erase. It has been said that what one learns in childhood is like something carved in stone. I say that this image is the basic cause of the differences of beliefs and the variety of tenets. . . .If the mothers are educated, know human rights, and what the precepts of honour and civilization require, there is no doubt that their children will adopt their characters and will acquire from them these virtues. I think that when women's education is neglected, then even if all the males of a nation are learned and high-minded, still the nation is able to survive in its acquired stage only for that generation. When they disappear, their children, who have the character and educational deficiencies of their mothers, betray them, and their nation returns to the state of ignorance and distress."[79]

In fact, Afghani points out, all the failures in the reformation of the Muslims are due to Muslim reformers' ignorance of the real nature of the problem. Reform needs a close study of several social, political, religious and historical processes which a nation has gone through. Only then could effective solutions of the problems which have arisen in a certain period be thought out and given a practical shape.[80]

References

1. *Cf.* pp. 68 below ff.
2. *'Urwah*, i, p. 86
3. ibid., ii, p. 87
4. ibid., ii, p. 66
5. ibid., i, p. 116
6. ibid.
7. *'Urwah*, i, p. 87
8. ibid., p. 88
9. *Cf.* Chapter IV
10. M, pp. 122-23
11. *'Urwah*, ii, p. 32
12. ibid., p. 30
13. ibid., pp. 7-8
14. *'Urwah*, 1, p. 194
15. ibid.
16. ibid., ii, pp. 161-62
17. ibid., p. 164
18. ibid., pp. 41-42
19. *Ta'rīkh*, ii, pp. 7-14
20. ibid., p. 11 : A striking resemblance exists between these views and that of Ibn Miskawaih. Ibn Miskawaih in his philosophical work *al-Fauz al-Aṣghar* (i.e. 'the smaller work on salvation'), while discussing the perfection and degradation of soul has elaborated on the social aspects of human life. He states that "man is by nature a social being. He cannot live without assistance from

his fellows. Consider, for instance, how he differs from the animals. Every animal has been endowed by his Maker with the necessary means of survival. There are the organs of offence and of defence, organs to secure food, and so forth. They have (i) an appropriate physical structure and (ii) they have also a natural instinct which is for them 'divine inspiration' and guidance. But man is different. He is born helpless in every sense of the term. A life-long dependence upon others is ordained for him. But he has Reason which animals are without. Hence he soon learns to supply his wants. He lives through rational coöperation with others. They serve and support him in his period of helplessness. He must do likewise. He must serve others just as they serve him. And this is but just. Only rational cooperation with others can ensure a just arrangement and continuity of human society." Khwaja Abdul Hamid, *Ibn Miskawaih, A Study of His Al-Fauz al-Asghar* (Lahore, 1946), pp. 50-51

21. ibid., pp. 11-12
22. ibid., p. 13
23. M, pp. 75-76 ff.
24, M, pp. 37-38
25. M, pp. 38-39
26. *'Urwah*, i, p. 191. See also pp. 70 below ff.
27. M, pp. 106-7
28. ibid., pp. 78-79
29. *'Urwah*, ii, p. 34
30. M, p. 149
31. ibid., p. 150
32. ibid.
33. ibid.
34. *Cf.* pp. 93 below ff. Also compare his views discussed above, pp. 33
35. M, p. 97
36. ibid., p. 33
37. H, pp. 74-79 ff.
38. R. Levy, *The Social Structure of Islam* (Cambridge, 1957), p. 459
39. *Tā'rīkh*, i, p. 51
40. M, p. 135
41. M, p. 136
42. M, pp. 136-37
43. ibid., p. 137
44. ibid., p. 89
45. ibid., p. 90
46. ibid., pp. 89-90
47. ibid.
48. Review of Buṭrus Bustāni's new Arabic Encyclopaedia, *Miṣr*, ii, no. 43, April 25, 1870. Eng. tr., *Biography*, pp. 106-7
49. ibid., pp. 114-15
50. ibid., p. 118
51. ibid., p. 95. A similar criticism is found in al-Ghazāli's *al-Munqidh min al-Ḍalāl*, where he states that it is customary with weaker intellect to take men

as criterion of the truth and not the truth as criterion of man." W. Montgomery Watt, *The Faith and Practice of Al-Ghazali* (Cambridge, 1957), pp. 39-40. At another place he says : "Wherever one ascribes a statement to an author whom they approve they accept it, even though it is false; wherever one ascribes it to an author of whom they disapprove, they reject it even though it is true. They always make the man the criterion of truth and not truth the criterion of the man; and that is erroneous in the extreme." ibid., p. 42

52. M, p. 95. Al-Ghazāli, in *Munqidh*, states : "A grievous crime indeed against religion has been committed by the man who imagines that Islam is defended by the denial of mathematical sciences, seeing that there is nothing in revealed truth opposed to these sciences by way of either negation or affirmation, and nothing in these sciences opposed to the truths of religion." Watt, op. cit., pp. 34-35; See also Levy, op. cit., pp. 503-4

53. M, p. 94

54. ibid.

55. ibid., pp. 147-48

56. ibid., pp. 91-92

57. ibid., pp. 134-35

58. ibid., p. 92

59. ibid., pp. 91-92

60. ibid., p. 93

61. ibid., pp. 92-93

62. ibid., pp. 134-48

63. ibid., pp. 29-30

64. M, art., "Falsafa-i- Waḥdat-i-Jinsīya wa Ḥaqīqat-i-Ittiḥād-i-Lughat," p. 77. See also Maḥmūd Qāsim, op. cit., p. 26

65 M, ibid.

66. ibid.

67. ibid., p. 70. In India Afghani described Urdu as the common language and advised the people to enrich it with words taken from Sanskrit, Marathi, and Bengali, and even English if necessary. Ibid , p. 80

68. ibid., pp. 78-80

69. ibid., pp. 80-82

70. ibid.

71. '*Urwah*, i, p. 65

72. ibid., p. 66

73. ibid., pp. 66-67

74. ibid., pp. 67-68

75. ibid., pp. 68-89

76. M, p. 92

77. Maghribi, op. cit., pp. 95-96

78. M, p. 93

79. Ḥakīm al-Sharq, *Miṣr*, 11, No. 47, May 24, 1879, quoted, *Biography*, pp. 110-11. Nevertheless, he was not in favour of unveiling of women for fear of moral degeneration in view of the existing social conditions of the Muslims. *Khāṭirāt* (Arabic), pp. 67-74

80. '*Urwah*, i, p. 64

THREE

MORAL VALUES

Afghani's ethical views are found in his analysis of the causes of the decay of Muslim community. One of the reasons underlying the backwardness of the Muslims is described by him as a deterioration of their moral standards. His treatment of morality is devoid of that discursive and didactic style which is generally employed by the few Muslim thinkers who wrote on essentially ethical problems. Among them the works of Ibn Miskawaih and al-Ghazali are recognized as authoritative texts of Muslim ethics.

It would be found that between these two, Afghani chose the former as more close to his point of view. In his approach a lack of emphasis on theological basis for moral values closely resembles the insistence on rational sanction for them in Ibn Miskawaih. Afghani's concept of morality has as its chief object the good of society as a whole. Consequently, his views on man's perfection, criterion of virtue and vice, nature of human emotions and the control of reason which they require, and the need of moral discipline for the maintenance of society follow the general line prescribed by Ibn Miskawaih. The latter's conception of morality and society would become clear by a passage from his *Tahdhīb al-Akhlāq*:

"There is a multiplicity of forms of happiness and no man alone can achieve them all. Men, therefore, must live together in societies in order to aid one another in attainment of them. Every good and every happiness indeed is derived from association, attaining perfection only in society, and when achieved it is common to all who have partaken in the effort leading to it. Each individual in the society helps the others as the members of the body help one another. True morality, then, is a social virtue, and is not to be attained by the solitary and the recluse."[1]

Indeed, the structure of Afghani's ethical system as a whole is based upon that of Ibn Miskawaih, although for certain matters he has drawn much from al-Ghazali. However, his ethics does not rely exclusively upon these two philosophers. Basing his theory upon them Afghani adds to it his own interpretation of morality and the practical aspects of moral conduct.

Regarding the development of individual personality he holds that unlike animals, who are born with instincts enabling them to know what is beneficial and what is harmful to them and to meet the needs of their lives, man is born without such instincts. "He is like a plain slate, a book with blank pages, or a land unploughed and uninhabited."[2] He adopts same thoughts, opinions, manners and the moral code which are followed by his parents and close relations.[3] For his mode of thinking, inclinations, passion for unfolding the mysteries of physical and metaphysical spheres, search into the secrets of the external phenomenon of life, he is indebted to the influences inherited from his parents and borrowed from the environment in which he is brought up.[4]

However, Afghani does not mean that man's thoughts and opinions are borrowed entirely from the environment and the persons around him. Man has two great faculties of reason and observation which are endowed by God to all human beings without any discrimination. By virtue of physical and mental faculties, they enjoy full freedom of will and action in order to achieve perfection (*kamāl*).[5]

The achievement of perfection, he points out, depends on man himself. It depends upon the full-fledged activity of the faculty of reason.[6] Reason is composed of observations and the knowledge attained through them. Each act of observation produces a corresponding thought, provoking an action which in its turn incites a new thought. In this way thought and action continue to influence each other as long as the relationship between soul and body continues to exist.[7] In view of the fact that observations, thought impressions, and will to act cause each other to originate, man stands responsible for his own actions. Here it is that Afghani brings in the need for a moral discipline. He argues that since each individual pursues his aims according to his own mode of thinking, natural instincts and inclinations, a clash among different individuals is imminent at any stage. Therefore, a system of principles is to be evolved which could avoid such conflicts. Such a system could not be other than having firm ethical foundations. Afghani holds that society is influenced by the thoughts and actions of individuals just as human nature is affected by the climatic changes. It is for this reason that God has sent prophets and revealed holy scriptures so that harmony in the thoughts and actions of individuals could be maintained and society saved from disintigration.[8] Like any natural phenomenon which obeys one or the other system of unalterable laws there exists a system of moral laws which must be followed strictly to attain the *summum bonum* of life-happiness (*Sa'ādat*).[9]

Afghani points out that the purpose of creation and of the system of natural laws is to make life easy and peaceful. Giving instances of physical and biological laws which govern the physical and biological world, he suggests that all these facts explain God's purpose of keeping life a going. In the same way ethical laws aim at the preservation of a peaceful society and the achievement of happiness for mankind at large. Deterioration of a society is directly the result of a fall in moral standards. When society does not follow the ethical principles in a rational way, it disintegrates.[10]

The basic issue of morality is the interpretation of virtue and vice. Afghani defines virtues (*faḍā'il*) and vices (*razā'il*) in the context of social utility of human actions. Thus, moral qualities which create love and unity among human beings are called virtues. Such virtues are thinking, freedom from superstition, nobility, loyalty, chastity, large-heartedness, love, respect for society, preference of the good of others to one's own, etc. Vices are those qualities which destory social relationship. These are immodesty, treachery, perfidy, hypocrisy, envy, pride, mischief-making, jesting, cowardice, etc.[11]

Virtues

Virtues purify and strengthen society. They unite individuals, make them act with the same impetus, obeying one single idea and having one common purpose. All virtues put together constitute justice (*'adl*). When justice is maintained in a society, then, each individual refrains from violating the rights of others. In this way equality and unity are preserved in a society.[12] Virtues occupy the same place in a society as life-force in human beings. Life-force gives each physical organ a power sufficient for its own functioning and not disturbing the functions of other organs. In the same way virtues restrict individual actions to certain limits. The prosperity, honour and strength of the whole society is assured when individuals share the gains of society attained by their own collective efforts.[13]

Vices

Vices lower men to the same extent as the virtues raise them in the eyes of society. Individuals, indulging in vices and sins, no longer remain faithful either to their nation or to themselves. Vices lower their morals, make them unmindful of their duties to and rights of their fellow-beings, family, tribe, nation and religion. In this way vices break the unity of a society.[14]

To regard love and unity as the only criteria in judging qualities as virtues or vices is a principle which points to a deep social insight on the part of Afghani. It also shows that he was conscious of the fact that moral discipline could be more appealing if it was based upon social foundations than described as a religious dogma.

He presses his point a little further by explaining the importance of reason in social activity. The faculty of reason plays an important role in attaining the two-fold object of satisfying natural desires and at the same time observing the welfare of society. He holds that, for the sake of society's existence and convenience in human livelihood, dispositions and habits must follow reason. Reason should control human desires and keep them within proper limits.[15] Then, following Aristotle's doctrine of the 'mean', he states that qualities serve as virtues when restrained within certain limits but when carried to excess, they turn into vices. So a middle position should be maintained. Al-Ghazāli in his *Iḥyā 'Ulūm al-Dīn* points out that excess or deficiency in qualities leads to vices, which occupy the extreme positions, while virtues lie in the middle, between the extremes.[16] The same view is held by Ibn Miskawaih.[17] Applying the principle of the mean, Afghani studies certain qualities as follows :[18]

Love of Life

Love of life, he holds, is the dynamic force behind all cultural phenomena. It inspires men to exercise all their energies to make life grand and rich with the wealth of fine arts and scientific discoveries. All cultural achievements, arts, crafts and scientific inventions are expressions of the love for life. It led man to the studies of the qualities of minerals, plants and animals, the nature of different kinds of lands and winds and movements of the stars. However, if this love for life is developed into love for one's own life it becomes a vice, makes man coward and humble and results into one's destruction.

Self-love

Self-love obliges a man to struggle for material comforts and honourable positions. This natural desire turns into a curse if exceeded beyond certain limits and makes a man selfish, who sacrifices the good of others for his own benefit.

Desire for Superiority over Others

The desire to become superior to others in all fields of life inspires men to learn all sciences and arts. If it is not checked this quality may develop into pride and envy. Man becomes proud only when in his ignorance he presumes that he has achieved perfection which, in fact, could not be attained except by incessant struggle and hard work. As a result of his pride he drifts away from his social circle and becomes useless for society. On the other hand, if he fails to satisfy his desire for superiority it changes into envy. Since envious men find themselves incompetent to equal the successful men, they concentrate their energies upon pointing out the defects of the latter and in obstructing their activities. Such persons gradually precipitate disruption in society.

Praise and Fame

Afghani remarks that usually men perform good deeds in order to satisfy their desire to be praised and to make a name for themselves. Such desire makes them act for common good and contributes towards the growth of sciences and arts for the benefit of society. All literary achievements and scientific discoveries are the product of such a desire. Again, it is for a lasting fame that great men sacrifice their lives for their country. However, if this desire is made an end in itself, it loses its real value. Anxious to get fame and praise, people allow themselves to practice hypocrisy, treachery, and deception. However, such an artificial fame produces no spiritual pleasure. It robs men of the spirit of struggle and labour and turns them into idle and useless beings.

Afghani points out that recognition of the noble deeds and condemnation of base actions invite people to act for common good in preference to individual gains. At the same time this acknowledgement of one's services for the society should not exceed its limits and develop into flattery. Undue praise and flattery might fill a man with vanity, make him ignore his defects and neglect the reformation of his conduct. Thus he would cease to be a useful member of society.[19]

Afghani states that there are persons who, regardless of their own good, act for the betterment of their country, nation and religion. Their whole lives are spent in hardships and spiritual sufferings. They have to suffer the wrath and opposition of even those persons who would ultimately be reaping the benefits of their struggle.[20] Afghani, however, maintains that it should not be supposed that these persons go through hell and fire for nothing. In fact, they have a natural desire to be praised by the grateful multitudes for whom they have gone through such hardships. This is the praise of a real and pure nature. The desire for real praise is like spiritual nourishment and psychological satisfaction for human nature. When a man reaches the height of perfection he puts aside petty desires and artificial comforts of baser sentiments and clings more closely to the passion for immortal fame and lasting praise. He leaves no stone unturned in performing great deeds in order to receive sincere commendation. The life of a virtuous man may be divided into two parts: one, which continues from his birth till his death, and the other, which begins by his first deed for the good of humanity and lasts till eternity. The former is confined to himself and the latter is retained in the hearts of the people for a long time. It is for this lasting life that the men of honour sacrifice their temporal pleasures. Such self-sacrificing personalities should come forward for the good of mankind. It is due to their brave and selfless deeds, which the others dare not accomplish, that a nation makes rapid advances in the spheres of science, morality, and culture.[21]

Love of Country, Nation and Religion

Patriotic, national, and religious sentiments also inspire men to compete with each other in the achievement of virtues and perfection. Such sentiments unify large groups of people to perform noble deeds, protect common rights and take action in defence of their country and religion. However, such sacred sentiments should not be overemphasized in which case they might deny truth and justice to the deserving, forfeit people's rights, and result in oppression against others.[22]

Optimistic Attitude towards Life

Among the moral qualities and sentiments which are helpful for individual as well as social welfare, Afghani lays great emphasis upon 'hope' as an attitude of life. On the other hand, despondency and despair act as poison for human energies and talents, since they hamper progress and lead a nation to destruction. A desperate man loses confidence in all his capabilities, degenerates morally, and surrenders to various kinds of humiliations. Such men lead miserable lives and do not object to working for the benefits of people who are totally alien to them and who fully exploit their weaknesses to their own advantage.

What could the cause of such despondency and pessimism be? According to Afghani it is due to a lack of faith in the omnipotence of God. The cause of human despondency, he holds, is that man wrongly regards his actions as emanating from his own power and will, and that he has full control over them. So, when a man experiences successive failures he feels that he is helpless and has no means to overcome the obstacles, and thus he turns desperate. On the other hand, if one has firm faith in an All-Powerful God who controls the universe and always comes to the succour of the faithful, then there is no room for despair or frustration.[23] Belief in God, thus, infuses in man an everlasting confidence which helps him in the achievement of high rewards, notwithstanding sufferings and hardships.

It is significant that throughout his discussion on morality Afghani lays great emphasis upon social values which must be kept in view while determining individual conduct as good or bad. This leads to the question: what should be the basis of the society where individual desires would be satisfied equitably, and secondly, what part do the moral values play in such a social set up? Afghani has discussed this issue in detail.[24] He suggests that there are four possible methods of keeping individual desires and ambitions under control for the security of the society; namely, force, nobility of soul, state authority, and religious faith.

Force

According to this method force is applied to safeguard human rights and to resist oppression. It would be tantamount to a reign of terrior if the mighty always dominated the weak. This would result in the destruction of human race.

Nobility of Soul

This method requires men to become spiritually noble and refrain from ignoble acts and qualities. Afghani points out that it is a well-known fact that the quality of the nobility of soul has no determined nature or specific value, which could universally be applied by different communities to control human desires and satisfy individual rights, and thus, to establish the foundation of a (social) system on firm grounds. It would be noted that certain qualities which are treated as ignoble by one community are treated as noble by the other. Theft and murder, for instance, are treated as noble qualities by the wild tribes, but are condemned by the civilized people. In the same way, treachery, cheating, and cunningness are looked upon as disgraceful by one community while for the other they stand for cleverness, perfection, and practical wisdom. Afghani explains very significantly that moral values are not followed absolutely for their own sake. In fact, man's desire to behave virtuously is nearly always motivated by the hope of extending his economic resources. Man acquires noble qualities, for he knows that if he is described by people as a noble person, he would have greater economic opportunities and a wider social circle. Besides, he would gain the confidence of others by the nobility of his character and would be considered trustworthy and righteous. On the other hand, a bad character is shunned by all and continues to lose his friends until even the resources of his livelihood are closed upon him. Thus, the desire for acquiring the quality of spiritual nobility, its strength or weakness, existence or non-existence and its different levels and stages and their influences, depend upon the economic conditions of different classes (of society). In other words, different classes of people try to attain this quality in as far as it benefits their livelihood and protects them from any harm or injury. In fact, each class utilizes this quality chiefly to safeguard its livelihood and to enhance its prestige. However, there are certain classes which do not regard the quality of spiritual nobility as worthy of acquiring, e.g. the rulers and the wealthy, who do not mind to behave in an ignoble way, especially with those who are inferior to them in position and status. They do not view their own actions as base or ignoble, whereas if anyone from amongst the common people behaves in this manner, he is accused by them of meanness and has consequently to suffer economic hardships. Ironically enough, none of the classes view the ignoble acts of the rulers and the wealthy as immoral. Instead, they try to interpret and justify them in some way or the other. Afghani states that the lower class receives such a treatment from the higher class for the simple reason that the latter feels quite immune and secure from the repercussions of its own immoral acts. Therefore, Afghani believes that if world administration is based upon the principle of spiritual nobility higher classes would continue to play their oppressive role over the lower classes and this would result in incessant tyranny upon the human race. Again, if, as described above, man is attracted towards noble deeds for the sake of material prosperity, then one cannot rule out that he might employ secret dealings, bribery, and other crooked means for achieving his objective. In view of the above facts, Afghani rejects moral discipline as an effective mothod of maintaining social peace. However, this mothod could succeed in its objective if it is sanctioned by a religion which has determined the essence of the nobility of soul in specific terms.

Authority of the State

The third method of protecting people's rights is the authority of the State. However, although the State could take action against blatant oppression, it is incapable of punishing the people engaged in conspiracies and secret dealings. Besides, the rulers and their officials themselves are men of low character and nothing could prevent them from following their base desires. If the State is made the protector of people's right, it would mean complete ruin of the defenceless and the poor. Hence, Afghani rejects this mothod as disastrous for social justice. He states that the only medium which could uphold common rights and protect people from the oppression of the powerful is religious faith.

Religious Faith

Belief in God and in reward and punishment are the fundamentals of religious faith. These two beliefs control base desires, eliminate external and internal oppressions, protect human rights, maintain peace, preserve soeial structure and culture and establish social transactions and economic affairs on firm foundations. Nothing but these two beliefs, especially, the belief in reward and punishment, could lead people towards virtue and restrain them from vice.

Afghani states that all world religions have furnished mankind with three beliefs (*'aqā'id*) and three qualities (*khaṣā'il*), which have helped individuals in the achievement of intellectual and spiritual perfection and have contributed towards the progress of society, world civilization, international relations, and towards the security of human race.[25] The three beliefs are:

1. "Man is the noblest of the creation of God." Afghani holds that one who has faith in this belief would naturally refrain from barbarous habits and bestial qualities which would be revolting to him. The deeper the roots of this belief the greater would be the disgust and man would advance in the sphere of reason and culture until he attains that state of life which is the ideal of the philosophers, namely, a life based upon love, wisdom, and justice. In short, such a belief restrains man from vices and along with his intellectual and rational faculties, leads him towards civilisation.

2. "His is the noblest nation." A man who has faith in this belief would struggle hard so that his nation may become equal with other nations of the world in every sphere of life whether it is spiritual, rational, or economic. He would never be prepared to see his nation in decay and misery while the other nations lead a prosperous and dignified life. Thus, such a belief is the most important factor for the overall progress of one's nation.

3. "Man has been created to attain perfection." Inspired by this belief man would try to adorn his reason with science and arts and give full expression to all of his inherent practical faculties, noble

thoughts and great qualities. He would keep his soul pure of base desires and earn his wealth through proper means and spend it in a proper way. This belief aims at establishing a civilization in which each individual has the knowledge of his rights and follows the straight path of justice.

The three qualities are: modesty (*ḥayā*), trust (*amānat*), and sincerity (*ṣadāqat*). Modesty is a feeling of remorse which the soul experiences on committing evil actions. Afghani holds that modesty restrains people from committing evil deeds more effectively than a number of laws and the police force. No punishment or sentence could prevent an immodest man from actions which create disruption in society. Social transactions, trust of promise and the honour of man depend on this quality. Modesty also represents pride (*nakhwat*) and honour (*ghairat*)—the two qualities which are the major reasons of intellectual and material progress of nations. Trust is the essence of mutual relations and social transactions among individuals. Afghani states that the administration of the social and economic affairs of a nation is looked after by its government, whether it is democratic, constitutional or despotic, through the organs of legislature, executive, judiciary, revenue and finance. He points out that the persons controlling these organs could serve society sincerely only if they possess the quality of trust. Otherwise, there would be no peace and security for the people or for their rights, loot and arson would reign supreme, the means of trade would be closed and the whole nation would ultimately be ruined. Thus the quality of trust maintains peace, unity and justice in a society.

In view of the fact that the needs of human livelihood are numerous and difficult to procure, man is obliged to seek cooperation and guidance of others. Such a cooperation, Afghani points out, could not be obtained unless the people are sincere to each other. Hence, sincerity is essential for a social organisation and for providing the means of livelihood for all.

The above analysis gives us a clear idea of Afghani's ethical outlook. He considers morality as a social necessity. Morality does not come foremost; it follows human nature. Describing happiness, in the Aristotelian manner, as the supreme end of human effort, Afghani emphasizes the fact that individual good rests in the good of the whole society. Morality functions as an effective system of principles which maintain a balance between individual ambitions and social obligations. Afghani describes ethical values as relative to the conditions prevailing in and the class structure of a society. Moral values change not only in different societies but among different classes of a single society, as well. However, society cannot function peacefully without some stable ethical foundation. It seems that Afghani was conscious of the fact that human behaviour could not be dictated by certain abstract moral principles. It was, perhaps, to avoid this obstacle that he lays down his own interpretation of virtues and vices which is purely utilitarian in character. According to this unorthodox definition those qualities which tend to unite individuals are virtues and those which cause disintegration in society are vices. It is significant that this interpretation lacks any special reference to theological sanction. Even when he specifies religion as the best among the means of bringing peace to society, he singles out the principle of reward and punishment, as the most important and relevant, chiefly because it has practical importance for ethical behaviour.

References

1. *Cf.* Levy, op. cit., p. 225
2. M, p. 113
3. ibid., p. 114
4. '*Urwah*, i, p. 87. *Cf.* Al-Ghazāli: "Training should be life-long and it should begin at birth, for then the child's mind is a precious jewel, free of all marks or figure. By education there can be engraved upon it all that is necessary to incline him either towards the good (which will give him happiness in this world and the next and bring him reward in which his parents and teachers share), or towards evil (indulgence in animal sloth), when he will be unhappy and perish". Levy, op. cit., p. 218
5. '*Urwah*, ii, p. 216; M, p. 115
6. Accodring to Ibn Miskawaih, "the best of men may be described as the man who performs persistently his own distinctive function, making use of his intellectual faculty as a means, and exercising his practical faculty so as to attain the end in view." D. M. Donaldson, *Studies in Muslim Ethics* (London, 1953), p. 128; See also Levy, op. cit., p. 228
7. '*Urwah*, i, p. 116
8. '*Urwah*, ii, p. 161
9. M, pp. 119-20
10. M, pp. 121-22
11. '*Urwah*, i, p. 191

12. ibid., p. 191

13. ibid., pp. 195-96. *Cf.* Ibn Miskawaih: "And if they (individuals) should agree at one time to work together in the quest of these many kinds of happiness, on the basis of mutual assistance (*mu 'awina*), then there would be many kinds of good attained in common (*al-Khairāt Mushtaraka*), and happiness would be something alloted or shared among them. They would rival one another for it, so that one would get part of it. In this way the perfection of mankind would be accomplished for all, by the help of all." Donaldson, op. cit., p. 124

14. ibid., p. 198

15. M, p. 123. Both Ibn Miskawaih and al-Ghazāli regarded reason as a counsellor to human desires. They used the Platonian illustration of the hunter who rides a horse and is accompanied by a hunting dog, to make clear the necessity of the rational-self retaining full authority over the other selves in the struggle for moral perfection. See for Ibn Miskawaih, Donaldson, op. cit., p. 129; for al-Ghazāli, *Cf.* Levy, op. cit., p. 216

16. Levy, ibid.

17. Donaldson, op. cit., p. 128

18. M, pp. 123-33

19. ibid., p. 13

20. '*Urwah*, ii, p. 66 ff.

21. ibid., p. 66

22. M, pp. 13-14

23. '*Urwah*, ii, pp. 34-37

24. H, pp. 63-74

25. H, pp. 21-37

FOUR

REFUTATION OF NATURALISTS

During his last sojourn in India (1879-1883), Afghani wrote a treatise entitled, *Ḥaqīqat-i-Madhhab-i-Nīchari wa Bayān-i-Ḥāl-i-Nīchariyān* (The Truth about the School of Naturalism and a Description of the Naturalists). An analysis of this work is necessary since it is the only detailed work of Afghani which contains his views on materialism and reflects certain fundamental aspects of his religious outlook.

Afghani was prompted to write this treatise, which is in a way a refutation of the views and beliefs of the naturalists, because of the growing popularization of the views of the school of Syed Ahmad Khan (1817—1898) better known as the founder of the M .A. O. College, which later developed into the Aligarh Muslim University. Muḥammad Wāṣil, a teacher of mathematics in the Madrasa-i-A'izza, Hyderabad, in a letter,[1] requested Afghani to explain the origin, aims and influence of the school of naturalism on human culture. He also sought to know the difference between naturalism and religion and whether naturalism supports religion or opposes it and what part does it play in civilization, culture and society.[2]

Afghani begins his treatise by stating that the *Nīchari* School (of India) was similar to the atheistic school that flourished in Greece during the third and the fourth centuries B.C. The real aim of this school was to uproot the foundations of all religions and establish *Ibāḥat* (rendering something lawful) and *ishtirāk* (communion) among the people.[3] He further states that the word *nīchariyat* (naturalism) was very popular in most of the cities of India and everyone gave a different interpretation according to his own understanding. However, people were ignorant of its true implications and meanings, and hence it was essential to give an account of naturalism from the very beginning and explain in detail the harm that they were causing to human society and culture. Again, it was necessary to prove rationally that wherever the protagonists of these views appeared, they caused decay and disintegration.[4] Later, in an article in *al-'Urwah*, Afghani states that during his stay in India he found that the Indian Muslims were led astray by the views of Syed Ahmad Khan as well as by his followers, and hence he wrote the treatise wherein, after describing the teachings of this false school and exposing their dangerous influences, he proved that religion was the only basis of civilization and culture.[5]

Before analysing the contents of the above treatise, it may be pointed out here that Afghani regarded Syed Ahmad Khan and his followers as materialists and atheists, and that this judgement seems to be unfounded and erroneous. It is, therefore, necessary to relate here the factors that led Afghani to such a conclusion.

At the time of Afghani's arrival in India (1879), the Indian Muslims had not recovered from the shock of frustration and defeatism which had overtaken them after the failure of the War of Independence in 1857. Besides, they were looked upon with suspicion by the British government. According to Afghani, the Indian Muslims, who had been deprived of their power and authority, had not become reconciled to the loss of their empire and that, as long as they were firm in their religious faith, it was not possible to make them acquiesce to foreign domination.[6] Further, in view of the growing activities of the Christian missions, the Muslims regarded English education as an indirect means to propagate Christianity. Hence, the Muslims became averse to Western culture on religious grounds. The majority of the orthodox *'Ulamā* took a firm stand against modern education and encouraged anti-British sentiments among the Muslims. Such an attitude and animosity threatened to deprive the Muslims of the government jobs which reqqired persons educated on modern pattern.

Syed Ahmad Khan, like the rest of the reformers of the period, saw that the Indian Muslims could regain their social stability, firstly, by inspiring confidence in the British government in India as to their loyalty,[7] and, secondly, by adopting Western modes of life and by acquiring modern education. Observing the aversion of the Muslims towards modern sciences on religious grounds, he held that there was need for a modern scholasticism so as to show that

Makhzūmi during his last days in Istanbul, sums up Afghani both as a believer and a rationalist, as follows:

"The gatherings of Afghani used to attract people of different faiths and diverse schools of thought. This made it necessary for him to address each person in a way suitable to his intelligence and preparedness, and to take into consideration his beliefs. He engaged in arguments those who would strip God of attributes, the materialists as well as biggoted divines. He expounded the philosophers, their writings and their systems; outlined their reasoning and conclusions.

"Thus opinions about him differed. Some considered him a renegade, others a religious fanatic. Many attributed to him the atheism found in some philosophical treatises. This was also the view held by common people of different sects who attended his gatherings and heard things they could not understand. Unconsciously they would transmit a distorted version of his teaching, proudly claiming to be his disciples and to have learned their unbelief (*kufr*) from him."[41]

References

1. *Biography*, pp. 15-16
2. *Documents*, plate 1, photo 2. *Biography*, pp. 37-38
3. *Documents*, plate 3, photo 9, Eng. tr. *Biography*, p. 54
4. *Risālah*, pp. 5-6, See also, E.G. Browne, *The Persian Revolution*, pp. 69-70; *Mashāhīr*, ii, p. 55; *Āthār*, pp. 69-70
5. Halil Fevzi, *Suyūf al-Qawāti* (Istanbul, 1870), summarized by Homa Pakdaman, *Djamal-ed-Din Assadabadi dit Afghani* (Paris, 1969), quoted, *Biography*, pp. 68-70
6. *Āthār*, p. 70
7. Halil Fewzi, op. cit., quoted, *Biography*, p. 73
8. *Biography*, pp. 75-80
9. ibid.
10. Ibrahim Makur, art., "Al-Farabi," in M.M. Sharif (ed.), *The History of Muslim Philosophy*, i, pp. 463-65; Luṭfi Jum'a, *Ta'rīkh al-Falāsafah al-Islam*, Urdu tr. (Hyderabad, 1941), pp. 47ff
11. Was born in 1823 and died in 1893. Among his works *Ibn Rushd* and *Ibn Rushdism, Origins of Christianity, History of the Israelites* and *Life of Jesus*, are well known
12. William G. Hutchinson, *The Poetry of Celtic Races and other Studies* (London, 1896), Introduction, p. x

13. ibid., p. 104

14. ibid.

15. For the English translation of the lecture, *Cf.* ibid., pp. 84ff. For its Urdu version, *Cf.* Qāḍi Aḥmad Miyān Akhtar Jūnāgadhi, *Islām aur 'Ilm* (Azamgarh, 1934), pp. 14ff.

16. Muhammad Hamidullah, "Ernest Renan and Jamal al-Din Afghani," *Islamic Review* (London, May, June, 1958), pp. 33 *et seq.*

17. *Zu'amā*, pp. 87-88. For the Urdu translation of the lecture, *Cf.* Qāḍi Aḥmad Miyān Akhtar, op. cit., pp. 43ff.

18. The original Arabic text is not traceable. For the Persian translation of the same, *Cf.* Murtaḍā, op. cit., pp. 54-62, which is based on the Arabic translation by Muhammad Hamidullah of the French version. For the French version see, Sayyid Jamal al-Din al-Afghani, *Refutation des Materialists,* by A.M. Goichon, Paris, 1942. For a summary in English see, *Biography,* pp. 190-195. A summary appears in *Zu'amā,* pp. 89-93; Muhammad Hamidullah, op. cit., pp. 33 *et seq.* In the beginning of his letter Afghani says that one of his friends had translated for him the article of Renan and that he would reply in Arabic. Its French version appeared in the *Journal des Debats* with a note by Renan that it was a faithful translation of the original Arabic text. M. Hamidullah, op. cit., p. 35

19. A.M. Goichon, op. cit., pp. 177-78

20. Here a reference should be made to a note by the Indian scholar Sayyid Ameer 'Ali who sought to refute this view of Renan by producing evidence to the effect that besides the above mentioned philosophers there were several other distinguished scholars who were Arabs by blood. Again, quoting passages from Renan's reply, he describes such criticism as "an insult to common sense and intelligence," *The Spirit of Islam* (Calcutta, 1902), pp. 424-29

21. A.M. Goichon, op, cit., pp. 178-85. Eng. tr. *Biography*, pp. 190-95

22. Hutchinson, op. cit., pp. 103ff. Renan states in a note to his reply: "A remarkably intelligent Afghan Sheikh, visiting Paris, having published in the *Journal des Debats* of May 18th 1883, some remarks upon the preceding lecture, I replied next day in the same journal as follows." ibid.

23. Hutchinson, op. cit., p. 104

24. Loc. cit., pp. 33ff.

25. Hutchinson, op. cit., pp. 100ff. Austin Henry Layard visited Mosul about 1845 for the excavation of Nineveh. A description of this visit is found in his *Nineveh and Its Remains* (London, 1949)

26. M. Hamidullah, op. cit., pp. 33-34

27. ibid., pp. 34-35

28. ibid., p. 35

29. *Zu'amā*, p. 89

30. *Encyclopaedia of Islam*, art., "Djemal al-Din Al-Afghani."

31. *Documents*, photos 138-140. For a description of this stand as anti-Islam see Elie Kedourie, *Afghani and Abduh : An Essay on Religious Unbelief and Political Activism in Modern Islam* (London, 1966), pp. 44-45

32. ibid.

33. *Zu'amā*, pp. 111-12

34. About five years earlier Afghani had said that the Muslims in their early period did not have any sciences but due to Islamic faith there was created among them a 'spirit of philosophy' which led them towards investigation of the affairs of the world and human requirements. This was the reason why they translated all sciences devoted to particular objects from Syriac, Persian and Greek into Arabic and mastered all such sciences in a short time during the period of Mansur Dawaniqi. *Risālah*, pp. 92-93. See also pp. 8 supra ff.

35. Statement of 'Abduh in Ṭāhir al-Tinali, (ed.), *Mudhākirāt al-Imām 'Abduh* (Cairo, 1961), pp. 34-36

36. Ibrāhīm Hilbāwi, "Ahamm Hadith Aththara fi Majrā Hayāti," *Al-Hilāl*, xxxviii, Dec., 1929, pp. 138-40; Anwar al-Jundi, *Al-Sharq fi Fajr al-Yaqzā* (Cairo, 1960), p. 20, quoted, *Biography*, p. 83

37. *Ta'rikh*, pp. 43-44

38. *Risālah*, pp. 11-13

39. A report submitted by Syed Husein to the British Resident in Hyderabad, Cordery, June 20, 1883, enclosed in F.O. 60/594, Cordery to India Office, June 25, 1883, quoted, *Biography*, pp. 144-45. Syed Husein's full name is Syed Ḥusain Bilgrāmi, 'Imādul Mulk, who was Secretary to Sālārjung II. This assessment is in sharp contrast with Afghani's image in his Hyderabad writings, particularly in his hard-hitting attack on Sir Syed's 'naturalism' which he equated with materialism and atheism. See Chapter 4

40. Maghribi, op. cit., pp. 35-36. It is to be noted that such accusations were made during the last days of Afghani's stay in Istanbul when due to his radical political views he had become suspicious in the eyes of the Sultan.

41. *Khāṭirāt* (Arabic), pp. 118-19. Eng. tr. in Sami A Hanna, "Al-Afghani: A Pioneer of Islamic Socialism," *Muslim World*, LVII, 1 (Jan., 1967), p. 25

EPILOGUE

How can Afghani be described? . . . as a fundamentalist, revivalist, reformer, modernist or non-conformist? In view of our study, it is difficult to do so. His definition of Islamic fundamentals, varying emphases on the revival of selected aspects of Islamic vision and refusal to conform to certain traditional concepts, invite the application of these terms variously or simultaneously. Does this signify any mutually contradictory elements in Afghani's thought, objectives and strategies? If so, how is it that these 'contradictory' positions appear to be sound when viewed independent of each other? Or, is there something wrong with our methodology itself? Let us probe this possibility.

What exactly do we understand by the terms fundamentalist, revivalist, reformer, modernist, non-conformist, etc.? Can a modernist not be a fundamentalist? What are the elements which distinguish a revivalist from a reformer? What a non-conformist does not conform to? Does a belief in the teachings enshrined in the Qur'an and the Ḥadith as constituting the fundamentals of a Muslim's religious life make a Muslim thinker a non-modernist? In what sense modernism is 'positive' and fundamentalism 'negative'? Let us ask, can a system exist and function without fundamentals? Unless the answer is negative, no assessment of Muslim thought and behaviour would be meaningful. To be sure, no Muslim or, say, Marxist can be discussed as such unless he has full faith in Islamic or Marxist fundamentals. In case a believer in Islamic fundamentals is taken as anti-modernism, it would imply that Islam itself is anti-modern and not anti-classical as in Iqbal's assessment. Extension of this assumption to the area of philosophy of religion would perforce render all considerations of modernism in the context of religious systems as futile and any believer whether Muslim or non-Muslim as non- or anti-modern.

Can we do that? Perhaps not, for the simple reason that we cannot afford to be too certain about the values to judge the validity of fundamentals. Certainty is an illusive objective for human reason to be achieved. It is un-scientific to do so. It is un-scientific and irrational to accept the scientific and the rational at a specific point of existence as totally certain. We are forced to exist on our contemporary assumptions of certainty.

We, therefore, are unable to do anything else than test the validity of values, through the experience of the past, in the context of contemporary knowledge. That is, the process of value-validity is not static but dynamic. Dynamism consists in validating a value-system on the basis of experience and knowledge accumulated by human mind at a particular point in time.

How about eternity of a value? Are there no eternal values in a system? Is a belief in the eternity of values a negation of dynamism of the process of value-validity? Is not, for instance, Truth an eternal value? No doubt, it is; what is not eternal is its definition. It is the definition or, rather, redefinition of an eternal value which explains the dynamism of this process. Thus, modernism consists in redefinition/re-interpretation of eternal values demanded by the accumulation of past experiences and knowledge, at a particular stage in human development. Modernism itself is a relative term: what is modernism today may be considered as conservatism in the 21st century.

Fundamentalism, does not mean to cling to the fundamentals as defined in the past, but to accept them in their essence. Seen from this angle, 'reformism' does not exist in Islam. Islamic fundamentals cannot be re-formed but only re-defined. Revivalism, similarly, does not mean revival of the fundamentals as they were defined in history but as they exist in the Qur'an. Revivalism would be negative or static if it stands for the revivalism of Islamic institutions as shaped in history. It is this attempt in the name of Islamic revival which has created unsurmountable problems for Islamic modernism. What is to be preserved is the eternal values of Islam as defined in the context of a given situation of experience and knowledge.

Afghani, with his refusal to be described by any of these terms, further confirms the desirability of a correct understanding of terms to be applied on Muslim thinkers, trends and movements. Afghani is neither a pure fundamentalist or a revivalist nor a modernist, since, as discussed above, the basic elements of these terms are not mutually exclusive. It is more appropriate to describe him simply as a modern Muslim intellectual. He was modern since he had experienced his Muslim past in the universal present in terms of contemporary knowledge. He was an intellectual as he knew how to use these two in a dynamic redefinition of the eternal values of Islam.

Afghani's stature as an intellectual is to be assessed in the context of changing Muslim societies of modern era. This era of multi-dimensional crisis ushered in by the consequences of the political and scientific might of the West was not favourable for the shaping of any comprehensive philosophical system addressed to the theological, social and intellectual aspects as, for instance, we find in Shah Waliullah of India of the 18th century. The crisis became complex due to its novelty. The chief distinguishing factor between the previous crises faced by Muslim society and the present one was that while the former emerged out of various theological, political and social cross-currents, within the Muslim ethos, the latter was a product of external political and cultural forces. Further, the crisis faced by Islamic theology due to the impact of Greek rationalism was not so grave and could be absorbed by the built-in philosophical and theological cushions used variously by the Mu'tazilites and the Ash'arites. On the other hand, this medieval Muslim intellectual tradition on which the 19th century Muslim mind had to rely, had no safeguards against the onslaught of the European culture powered by rationalism and science. The new crisis demanded quite a new approach for its analysis helpful in the protection of essential values of Islamic culture. However, the process of unfolding of this crisis was too fast to allow time and peace for the Muslim (in fact, the Eastern) peoples even to assess the exact nature of the spiritual, intellectual and material implications of Western culture for Islam and Muslim societies. This explains the partial nature of Muslim responses to Western challenges during the last one hundred years or so. In Afghani we find the first indications of a philosophic awareness of the new crisis and of a dynamic approach to tackle it.

Afghani's intellectual response was governed mainly by the problems created by the political and intellectual thought of the West and its political forms. He probably did not think and proceed as he would have desired to do; he was forced by the immediate crises to be selective in the ordering of his priorities. Nevertheless, his philosophical premises scattered in his writings and recorded by his companions and the practical steps which he took, provide us with his conceptual framework for reconstruction of Islamic thought.

The most important feature of this approach is evident in the transfer of emphasis from abstract theory of Islam to Muslim society as such. It was the material (political, social and economic) decline and stagnation of Muslim peoples which led him to re-examine the philosophical content of those Islamic concepts which governed the cultural aspects of life. It is, thus, no mere accident that Afghani deals more with those Islamic beliefs and concepts which are directly or indirectly related to social realities than with Islamic metaphysics, mysticism or purely philosophical issues. He believed that the political and intellectual stagnation of the 19th century Muslim world was the logical result of the neglect of true Islamic principles during the previous five or six centuries and, therefore, its survival lay in rediscovering the true fundamentals of Islam. The preceding movements of religious reform, namely, the *Wahhābiya* and the *Sanūsiya*, had a limited scope. While their call to restore Muslim society to its prestine purity had a universal appeal, their political interests were confined to Nejd and al-Maghrib. Afghani inherited from the *Wahhābiya* the doctrine of purity of faith; but whereas the former considered the basis of pure Islam to be metaphysical, Afghani described it as social. For the *Wahhābiya* the chief danger lay in innovation—an internal phenomenon, while for Afghani the main danger emanated from the West and the prejudiced outlook of the Muslims towards modern knowledge. He was fully aware that the religious and political battles against the West could be fought and won only in the intellectual field. Unless the Muslims re-established religion on reason and science they would not be able to keep up with the rapid advances of history. The Mu'tazilites in a way held the same approach; but while for them it was purely a philosophical problem, for Afghani it was an existential one.

The Muslim society as observed by Afghani did not consist merely of the rulers, the '*Ulamā* or the rich; it was of the Muslim masses—the down-trodden majority at the mercy of the few rich and the powerful. He found Muslim societies whether in Muslim areas (the Arab, Turkish or Iranian regions) or areas of strong

Muslim minorities (like India) persecuted by the rich, the absolute monarchs and Western imperialists and restrained in progress by their distorted image of Islam and intellectual backwardness. Muslim society, therefore, was stagnant due to three factors, namely, absolute dictatorship (*istibdād*), distorted religious faith and biased view (*ta'aṣṣub*) of knowledge. These three, in his opinion, have no place in the Islamic view of life. Quoting the *Qur'an* and citing examples from Muslim history, he condemned all forms of suppression. He exposed the ignorance of *'Ulamā* and their failing in their duty of providing guidance to the peoples. Thirdly he brushed aside the traditional division of knowledge into Muslim and non-muslim categories, an error which, he held, was responsible for intellectual stagnation of Muslims for the last five hundred years. Such was Afghani's diagnosis of Muslim problems and identification of those responsible for their creation.

The question was how to deal with this complex situation. Since the issues were of philosophical, political and social nature with deep inter-linked roots in the historical tradition, no single plan of action could be effective. A man of action himself, Afghani knew it. In his final analysis which he appears to have made around 1884 (when he published *al-'Urwah*) he selected following steps in his plan of action:

(A) *Theoretical*

(i) to offer an interpretation of Islam, through a critical examination of Islamic historical tradition removing all theological empediments in the way of social and intellectual progress.

(ii) to expose the distortions and misinterpretations in beliefs and practices in medieval Islamic theology and the misguidance of the *'Ulamā* of his age.

(iii) to make the Muslims, chiefly the Muslim youth, aware of the urgent need of acquiring modern knowledge as an essential condition for progress.

(B) *Operational*

(iv) to start a movement among the Muslims for political modernisation, that is, establishment of constitutional governments instead of monarchy and for *Waḥdat al Islāmia*. While the former would provide popular governments required for speedy social

> reforms, the latter would help create an atmosphere of religio-political coordination among the Muslim countries for meeting European military threats and for united action for common social and educational reforms.

So far as the theoretical aspect is concerned, Afghani prefaces his interpretation of Islam with a justification for a religious system. Religion, according to him, served chiefly as a system to maintain peace in society and aimed at the achievement of happiness for all individuals. The other institutions used for the same objective are state and morality. State, based on force, can never he relied upon as there is every possibility of its being misused by evil persons. Even a moral system has no absolute values of its own; it is, in fact, a social code of human behaviour, changing according to the interests of different classes and cultural traditions of a society. Religion, on the other hand, aims at maintaining social peace through certain beliefs containing everlasting moral values. Afghani identifies the beliefs in God and reward and punishment as basic to all religious systems. The former belief helps man to maintain his spiritual personality and the latter, as a moral restraint, preserves social peace. Islam is the best upholder of these eternal values and provides full scope for intellectual and material uplift of the individual in the interest of whole society. Science, according to Afghani, is not a rival but a component of Islamic spirituality. For social organisation Islam provides a moral value-system based on the beliefs in unity of God and the Day of Judgement. Islamic political system is democratic in spirit having no room for hereditary monarchy or dictatorship. Muslim society has to be governed by law and not by arbitrary human will. As a logical outcome of this interpretation, Islamic legal system has to keep pace with social change and liberate itself from the rigidities of various schools of law which had tied down the Muslims during the past several centuries. Through the dynamic principle of *ijtihād*, Afghani paves the way for the formulation of laws according to the social needs of every age. What come into conflict with ever changing social values are not the eternal fundamental beliefs of Islam but the legal systems which came into being in response to the needs of society at various stages in the past. Therefore, *ijtihād* may be resorted to for new legislation wherever required for keeping

Muslim society moving. His deep concern over the ever growing pressures of social change is reflected in his views on the need of preparing a new Qur'anic commentary which, he emphasizes, should be oriented to the new social, political and philosophical problems and written by one who is well-versed in both Islamic and western sciences.

Such interpretation of religion as a social system was quite new to the 19th century Muslim mind which continued to treat religion as a purely spiritual and rigid legal system. Afghani suggested the study of this issue from a philosophical angle. His belief that without the spirit of philosophy no society can progress is, in fact, a demand for acquiring a mental attitude in which the spirit does not dominate the rest but is complementary to the material part of human life. As such, religion would serve not as an end in itself but as a means to achieve happiness for human beings. Generally, the Muslims did not seem to have a clear idea of the role of knowledge in the evolution of society. It was Afghani who, for the first time, realized that science has emerged as a more relevant source of power and progress. In fact, he appears to believe that science is destined to play a more decisive role in human affairs in future than metaphysics. He points out that the powerful political structure and material prosperity of Europe was based upon its superior scientific knowledge. He, therefore, considered the learning of modern sciences by the Muslims as a prerequisite for revival of early purity of Islam.

The pressures of western imperialism, especially of the British, had become so intense that no long-term plan for religious reform and intellectual renaissance could be initiated without tackling the political question first. The west was ready to take advantage of the political dissensions among the Muslim rulers. Hence, Afghani advocated the establishment of constitutional governments in Muslim countries and appealed for the unity of Muslim countries under a single caliph.

However, there were three chief obstacles in the achievement of Muslim renaissance: (a) foreign political pressures, (b) despotism of Muslim rulers, and (c) the orthodox *'Ulamā* who in order to safeguard their religious prestige and political influence supported the reactionary policies of the rulers. Afghani found that the factor which would decide the future of the Muslim world was the outcome of the struggle between the enlightened Muslims (mostly under the influence of European sciences and institutions) and the orthodox section of the *'Ulamā*, both of whom took the support of religion to put forward their conflicting points of view. Afghani could not subscribe to anyone of these views to the exclusion of the other. The enlightened section of Muslims with all its progressive ideas was not sufficiently influential, while the *'Ulamā* who were more powerful, suffered from a prejudiced outlook. Afghani, therefore, struck a balance between the two points of view and at the same time presented his own interpretation of Islam as a functional social system. He held religion as the spirit and science as the strength of Islamic culture. On the one hand, he acknowledged the importance of the *'Ulamā* as a theological assistance against the absolutism of Muslim rulers (as they served in Iran) and, on the other hand, made their opposition to western thought ineffective by arguing that modern sciences were not against the precepts of Islam. As regards the enlightened Muslims, who served as the backbone of his reformative programme, he organized them around his dynamic theme of religious reconstruction on the foundations of modern sciences and, at the same time, restrained them from over-rationalizing religious beliefs, which might minimize the spiritual values of religion.

It was this wide-ranging struggle against Western imperialism, Muslim despots and the orthodox out look, which invited bitter opposition from his far more powerful enemies who deprived him of every opportunity to give effect to his plans of Muslim renaissance.

However, his thought left a deep impress upon the contemporary and later Muslim intellectuals and religious and political leaders.[1] In Persia, the political aspect of his religious thought was taken up by most of the political leaders and the *'Ulamā* of his time and was manifested in the national movement culminating in the revolution of 1905-1906.[2] Among them the most distinguished were Mirza Naṣrullah Malik al-Mutakallimīn,[3] Shaikh Hādi Najmābādi,[4] Sayyid Muḥammad Ṭabāṭabāi,[5] Āqā Khan Kirmāni,[6] and Shaikh Āḥmad Rooḥi.[7] Afghani's Pan-Islamic ideology and anti-West tendencies continued to find expression among the writings of the later literary figures of Persia.[8] In Turkey, the Young Turk movement might be said to have followed anti-Hamidian, Pan-Islamic and liberal policies similar to those of Afghani.[9] In India Maulana Abul Kalām Āzād and the poet-thinker Iqbāl, among others, were deeply influenced by his diagnosis of the degeneration of Muslims as well as by his views on religious reforms.[10] In Egypt, where his stay was longer than in any other country, his religious mission was more systematically and effectively carried forward by his distinguished disciple Muḥammad 'Abduh and the *al-Manār* party.[11] 'Abdul Raḥman al-Kawākibi (1849-1903) of Syria was a disciple of Afghani and derived the substance and form of his theory of Arab nationalism from Afghani's religious and more comprehensive political ideology.[12] In Russia, Ismā'il Bey Gasprinsky (1851-1914), the most outstanding figure in the history of Russian Turks in the 19th century,[13] and the Azerbaijani leaders, such as Resul Zadeh, Topchibasheve and Agaeve, were deeply influenced by Afghani.[14] However, in the early part of the 20th century, Pan-Islamism received a set-back due to the emergence of nationalist movements which, in a way, ran counter to Afghani's concept of the unity of Muslim peoples. The movements of Pan-Turanism and Turkish nationalism produced a parallel reaction among the Arabs. These movements were based on the conception of race, language and culture rather than on religion.

Afghani had succeeded in stirring the religious and political life of the Muslims of his time. He was respected by the people, feared by the Muslim rulers, and hated by the reactionary '*Ulamā*. Britain tried to exploit his influence in the settlement of the Egyptian question and the Mahdi uprising in Sudan, but, all the same, he was treated as a dangerous agitator. The '*Ulamā* condemned him as the advocate of rationalism. The Muslim rulers, like Sultan 'Abdul Ḥamīd II of Turkey and Nāṣiruddin Shah of Persia, tried to use his influence in order to advance their own political interests and to pacify the growing national awakening in their own countries. But, as soon as they discovered that his ideas of reforms went counter to their despotic authority they disowned him. He was exiled from Persia and Egypt and was put under house-arrest by Sultan 'Abdul Ḥamīd in Turkey.

The failure to move the rulers and the '*Ulamā*, who were the accredited leaders of the Muslims, to associate themselves with his movement of religious and political revival, disappointed Afghani. As a result he turned more and more towards the masses. He exhorted them to rise in revolt against their own corrupt rulers. In the last days of his life he wrote a letter to his colleagues in Persia in which he said:[15]

> "Only on this account am I grieved, that I have not lived to reap what I have sown, and that I have not fully attained to that which I desired. The sword of unrighteousness has not suffered me to see the awakening of the peoples of the East and the hand of ignorance has not granted me the opportunity to hear the call of Freedom from the throats of the nations of the Orient. Would that I had sown all the seeds of my ideas in the receptive ground of the people's thoughts . . . . You, who are the ripe fruit of Persia, and who have zealously girded up your skirts for the awakening of the Persian, fear neither imprisonment nor slaughter. Be not frightened by the ferocious acts of the Sultans. Strive with utmost speed, and endeavour with the greatest swiftness. Nature is your friend, and the Creator of Nature your ally. The stream of renovation flows quickly towards the East."

As correctly assessed by Fazlur Rahman, "the most salient feature of his spiritual attitude, which he has bequethed to the Modernist Muslim, is his unbounded humanism. Indeed, there is evidence to the effect that even his appreciation of religion was based upon a a humanist *elan*; for religion, including Islam, according to him served human ends. It, therefore, must be concluded that his emphasis on populism was not just a means to an external end, the strengthening of Muslim governments against a foreign enemy, but was possessed of intrinsic value. Indeed Afghani appears to be the sympathetic advocate of the downtrodden and the deprived".[16]

References

1. Wilfred Cantwell Smith says: "There is very little in twentieth century Islam not foreshadowed in Afghani." *Islam in Modern History* (Princeton, 1957), p. 48

2. For his personal influence among the elite and the masses in Persia, *Cf.* the statement of Riḍā Kirmāni, TBI, p. 83; E. G. Browne, *The Persian Revolution*, p. 73. Nāzim al-Islām Kirmāni mentions several *'Ulamā*, officials and traders who came under Afghani's influence and played a vital role in the

Persian national movement. TBI, pp. 63-64, 155. See also, *Sharh*, pp. 58, 83; Malikzadeh, op. cit., pp. 179, 212-14, 258; *Ḥayāt-i-Yaḥyā*, p. 98; TBI, p. 155; E. G. Browne, op. cit., p. 415; Ahmad Kisravi, *Ta'rīkh-i Mashrūtiyat-i Iran* (Tehran, 1330, Solar), pp. 10, 12, 14-15, 136, 139

3. Malikzadeh, op. cit., p. 191

4. E.G. Browne, op. cit., pp. 82, 406; Murtaḍā, op. cit., p. 66

5. TBI, pp. 49-50

6. ibid., pp. 148-50, E. G. Browne, op. cit., pp. 409-14

7. E.G. Browne, op. cit., p. 415; TBI, p. 155

8. *Cf.* Isḥāque, *Modern Persian Poetry* (Calcutta, 1943), pp. 142ff.

9. Afghani has remained as a source of inspiration to certain distinguished figures of Turkey. For instance, Shināsi (1826-1871), the founder of Tanzimat literature, was an intimate friend of Afghani. *Cf.* Halide Edib, *Conflict of East and West in Turkey*, 2nd edition (Lahore, 1935), pp. 185-86. Ziyā Gokalp, the theorist of Turkish nationalism, and the nationalist poet Mehmet Amin were also inspired by Afghani's ideas. *Cf.* Uriel Heyd, *Foundations of Turkish Nationalism* (London, 1950), p. 108. See also Kemal H. Karpat, *Turkey's Politics: The Transition to a Multi Party System* (Princeton, New Jersey, 1959), p. 30n. 62, 63, 90. It is also reported that Afghani was an associate member of the Bektashi Order of Darvishes, which cooperated with the Young Turks in their anti-Hamidian struggle and were accused by the orthodox '*Ulamā* for their religious liberalism. *Cf.* Duckett Ferriman, *Turkey and the Turks* (London, 1911), p. 202

10. In the beginning of the 20th century Maulānā Āzād started a weekly journal *al-Hilāl* exactly on the pattern of *al'Urwah al-Wuthqā*. The early issues of this journal published several articles on Afghani's life and career and his views of religious reforms were highly praised. Iqbal's works, especially his *Reconstruction of Religious Thought in Islam*, and *Jāwīd Nāmah*, vividly exhibit his devotion to Afghani's religious ideas. For Afghani's influence on the Indian Muslims, *Cf.* the collection of articles on Afghani by eminent Muslim scholars of India, *Maqām-i-Jamāl al-Dīn Afghani*, by Sayyid Mubāriz al-Dīn Raf'at (Karachi, 1948). See also Aziz Ahmed, *Studies in Islamic Culture in the Indian Environment* (Oxford, 1964), Chap. 4

11. *Cf.* The excellent work on Muḥammad 'Abduh, *Islam and Modernism in Egypt*, by C.C. Adams (London, 1933).

12. Hazem Zaki Nuseibeh, *The Ideas of Arab Nationalism* (New York, 1956), pp. 47-48; George Antonius, *The Arab Awakening* (London 1945), p. 97

13. Serge A. Zenkovsky, *Pan-Turkism and Islam in Russia* (Cambridge 1960), pp. 30ff.

14. ibid., pp. 271-72

15. E.G. Browne, op. cit., pp. 28-29

16. *The Cambridge History of Islam*, art., "Revival & Reform in Islam," ed. P. M. Holt, Ann K. S. Lambton & Bernard Lewis, Vol. 2B (Cambridge, 1970), pp. 62-43

APPENDIX

AFGHANI'S LIFE AND ACTIVITIES: A SYNOPSIS

Sha'bān, 1254 A.H./October-November, 1838

Birth

Determination of the country of his birth has remained a controversial issue. According to one set of evidences, he was born in As'adābād, Afghanistan, and according to the other, in Asadābād, Iran. Afghani himself has always stated that he was an Afghan and has signed himself either as "Jamāl al-Din al-Ḥusaini al-Afghani" or "Jamāl al-Dīn al-Ḥusaini". Some of his close associates and disciples held him as an Afghan.[1] On the other hand, several Persian sources support the view that he was born in As'adābād, near Hamadan in Iran.[2] According to this opinion Afghani's family was originally Persian and lived at Asadābād and later Afghani travelled to Afghanistan. Evidence to this view is equally weighty. Afghani, aware of this controversy, is reported to have told one of his disciples, Burhān al-Dīn Qalīj Khān, during his last years in Constantinople, that he was an Afghan by birth. He explained that the Iranians deliberately or otherwise mistook him as an Irani since another Shaikh Jamal al-Din, who was as Irani and a *Bābi*, visited all those places in Iran where Afghani had travelled.[3] Regarding Afghani's assertions that he was an Afghan, Nikki R. Keddie holds that he deliberately concealed his Iranian origin "to present himself to the Muslim world as a Sunni rather than a Shi'i, as the Sunnis formed the majority of Muslims outside Iran, while a Muslim ethnic Persian from Iran would be recognized as almost surely a Shi'i."[4]

Childhood and Early Education

Difference of opinion as to the country he lived in during his early years of education persists.[5]

1856-57

First visit to India. Visit lasted for one year and some months[6] or for four years,[7] during which he visited several cities and acquainted himself with modern European sciences. In the same year, 1273/1856-57, he visited Mecca for pilgrimage[8] and is also reported to have travelled to Iraq, Persia, Baluchistan[9] and probably Istanbul.[10]

1857—1868-69

(i) Account of supporters of his Afghanistan origin: He entered the service of Amir Dost Muḥammad Khān, the ruler of Afghanistan,[11] and after his death that of Sher 'Ali. As adviser to Sher 'Ali, he is reported to have introduced many reforms in administration: systematized the procedures of court, reorganised army, founded military schools, hospitals, schools, got postage-stamps printed and constructed roads and travellers' lodges.[12] Due to the treacherous role played by the Prime Minister, Rafique Khān left for India in 1282/1865-66.[13] Returned after about a year to serve under the new Amir, Muḥammad A'zam. However, the political conditions got unstable and he left Kabul for good in 1285/1868-69.[14]

(ii) Account of supporters of his Iran origin: This account supported by Afghani's personal papers rules out Afghani's stay in Afghanistan earlier than 1866.[15] According to it, there is no reliable information on Afghani's activities from 1858-1865. Definite earliest presence in Afghanistan is since 1866. He was adviser to A'zam Khan in 1867-68.[16] Exiled from Qandhār on December 11, 1868 and left for Bombay.[17]

1869

In India, for a month or from March-April to July, 1869. Proceeded to Cairo where he stayed for about (40) days, during which he met the '*Ulamā* and visited Azhar. Lectured on Ibn Sina's *Ishārāt*.[18] Left for Constantinople.

1869—71

Constantinople: Afghani received with respect by high government officials like the Prime Minister, 'Āli Pāshā, Fuād Pāshā and Munīf Effendi, President of *Anjuman-e-Ma'ārif* (Academy of Sciences). Was made a member of the Academy. Took interest in educational reforms. His views and suggestions welcomed by reformer-statesmen like 'Āli Pāshā and Fuād Pāshā, but opposed by the conservatives led by the *Shaikh al-Islām*, Ḥasan Fahmi Effendi.[19] Invited to speak at the inauguration of the new University, *Dār al-Funūn*, by Taḥsīn Effendi, the Director of the University. Delivered a lecture in *Ramaḍān*/November-December, 1870, on Arts.[20] Text of the lecture was approved by Turkish officials. His views expressed in the lecture attacked by the orthodox circles, led by Ḥasan Fahmi Effendi, as heretical. Campaign against Afghani. Government asked him to leave Constantinople. Left for Egypt.

At Constantinople: First public appearance as a reformer and liberal intellectual and first public attack by orthodoxy.

1871—79: Egypt

Arrived in Cairo in *Muḥarram*, 1288,[21] March 22, 1871.[22] Egyptian Prime Minister, Riyāḍ Pāshā, conferred stipend of about one thousand *qursh* (ten Egyptian pounds) per month not for any specific services but as token of respect to an illustrious visitor.[23] Became immediately popular among the students and the youth. Lectured on various subjects like mysticism, jurisprudence, scholasticism and physical and rational sciences. First indication of his thinking on uniting the Muslims of India, Afghanistan, Bukhara, etc., on the basis of Islam (*Ittiḥād-i-Islāmiya*) against Russia.[24] Stressed on intellectual and political awakening of Egyptian youth. For this purpose, encouraged starting journals like *Miṣr* and *al-Tijārah*.[25] Himself contributed to these journals. Most probably, wrote his *Tatimmah al-Bayān fi Tā'rikh al-Afghan*, here. Founded *al-Ḥizab al-Watani* (the nationalist party) for the social betterment, spiritual purification and political awakening of the Egyptian people.[26] Was attracted by Freemasonry and joined a lodge.[27] In 1876-79 became Grand Master of the Masonic Lodge of Alexandria.[28] However, disassociated himself later finding it not useful for his purposes.[29] Afghani and his group worked successfully for the deposition of Khedive Ismāil in favour of his son Tawfīq. Khedive Tawfīq, contrary to his earlier assurances to Afghani, apprehensive of the latter's persistant demands of political reforms and under pressure of Britain and France, expelled him. Afghani and his disciple Abu Turāb arrested on *Ramaḍān* 6, 1296/August 27, 1979.[30] Afghani left Egypt in September, 1879.[31]

Impact: Created great impression on the youth and intellectuals as a liberal thinker and political leader. Inspired them to study Islam independent of past authorities, to learn modern sciences and philosophy and to struggle for constitutional government. Faced opposition of the orthodox circles who accused him of holding unorthodox and even heretical views.[32] Succeeded in creating a group of young intellectuals which paved the way for the future religious reform movement, *Salafia*, and Egyptian nationalist movement. Shaikh Muḥammad 'Abduh, the most prominent among his disciples, later emerged as an outstanding Muslim thinker of modern age.[33]

1879—1882 : India

Reached Bombay via Karachi. After a brief stay in Bombay proceeded to Hyderābād, the capital of the Nizam's State, the largest Muslim princely state of India. Was surrounded by opponents of Sir Syed Aḥmad Khān of 'Aligarh. Was very active in writing in Persian. Wrote his treatise, "*Ḥaqiqat-i-Madhhab-i-Nīchari wa Bayān-i-Ḥāl-i-Nīcharyān*" (Refutation of Naturalists), against, what he considered to be, the naturalist thought of Syed Aḥmad Khān and his companions. Wrote almost all of his available Persian articles, covering a wide range of issues like the rise and fall of Islam and Muslims, the negative role of *'Ulamā*, importance of learning modern sciences and philosophy, language as a unifying force in a nation, etc. Was instrumental in starting jurnals, *Mu'allim* (edited by Sajjād Mirza) and, *Mu'allim-e-Shafīq* (edited by Muḥib-e-Ḥusain), from Hyderabad. Did not participate in any political activities, although his anti-British views can be clearly noticed in his articles camoflouged in metaphors and in his sarcastic references to those loyal to Indian British government. Was kept under watch by the government and then in late 1881 taken to Calcutta.[34] In Calcutta also he formed a small circle of admirers. Wrote some articles and delivered a lecture at Albert Hall, *Madrasa-e-'Āliya*:[35]

His movements watched by the government.[36] Left Calcutta in late 1882.

1883—85: Paris, London

Arrived in London in January, 1883. Met Wilfrid Scawen Blunt. Wrote his first two political articles, "English Policy in Eastern Countries", and, "The Reasons for the War in Egypt", published in the Bee/*al-Naḥla*, London, edited by Louis Sambunji. Contributed "Letter on India", to the French journal, *La Justice*. These articles criticised British policy in Egypt, Afghanistan and India and favoured Sultan 'Abdul Ḥamīd's policy of uniting the Muslims.[37]

Went to Paris during the same month of January, 1883. Wrote an article, *al-Sharq wa al-Sharqiyīn*" (the East and the Easterners) in Abu Nazzāra Zarqā', edited by James Sanua. *Waḥdat al-Islāmiya* became the central theme of his writings. His Egyptian disciples, including 'Abduh, re-established contacts with him through letters.

'Abduh translated Afghani's treatise on Indian Naturalists into Arabic entitled *al-Radd 'al al-Dahriyin.*

Afghani wrote his rejoinder to Ernest Renan's article on 'Islam and Science'. Both were published in *Journal Des Debats*. Was involved in the Mahdi uprising in Sudan against Britain. Wrote articles in *l' Intransigeant* on the Mahdi, welcoming this movement as a means of uniting Muslims on the basis of Islam against foreign colonialists and imperialists, particularly Britain.

'Abduh joined Afghani in 1883. Afghani met Victor Hugo and Olivier Pain.[38]

Journal *al-'Urwah al-Wuth qa*, edited by Afghani and 'Abduh, started in 1884 probably as the organ of a society, *Jami'at al-'Urwah al-Wuthqa.*[39] The title of the Journal was taken from the Qur'anic verse, 'So whosoever disbelieves in the devil believes in Allah, he indeed lays hold on the firmest handle which shall never break'. (2.56). It published articles and comments reflecting as a whole the views of Afghani. Some of the important themes and subjects discussed were: domination of the West over the East, particularly that of England over the Muslim lands and India; Mahdi of Sudan; Russian threat to Afghanistan; Islamic teachings; importance of modern sciences; Islamic theological and ethical concepts of social and political significance; comparative study of Christianity and Islam and the rise of the Christians and decline of the Muslims; Free will and Pre-Destination; Vices and Virtues; dynamism of Qur'anic teachings; criticism of Muslim monarchs; Islamic unity (*Waḥdat al-Islāmiya*), etc.

'Abduh left at the end of 1884 for Tunis.

Talks with British government through W.S. Blunt on steps to solve the problem of British involvement in Mahdi uprising in Sudan with the mediation of Afghani. Talks failed. Attempt to prepare a scheme of aliance between England, Turkey, Iran and Afghanistan against Russia.[40] Contact between Afghani and Sultan Abdul Hamid established through emissaries. Afghani supported the Sultan as the symbol of Muslim unity.[41]

1886-87: Iran and Russia[42]

Iran (1886-87): Left London and reached Būshahr in May, 1886, where he stayed for six months. Met Malik al-Mutakallimīn, later one of the leading figures in the Iranian constitutional movement, Mirzā Furṣat al-Dawlah Shīrāzi and Mirzā Riḍā Kirmāni, who later, in 1896, assassinated Nāṣiruddīn Shāh, the king of Iran. On invitation received through I'temād al-Saltanah, Minister of Press and Publication, Afghani left for Tehran to see Naṣiruddīn Shāh Qāchār, via Shīrāz and Iṣfahān. In Iṣfahān, he met Hāji Sayyāḥ and Zil al-Sultān, the Shāh's eldest son and Governor of Iṣfahān. In Tehran, Afghani met the Shah. The Shah got suspicious of him because of his fearless manner and his strong views on reforms. He was forced to leave Iran.

Russia, (1883-89): May, 1887, arrived in Moscow. Visit arranged by Katkov, the editor of *Moscow Gazette*, who probably died the same year. Maharaja Dalip Singh, son of Ranjeet Singh, deposed in 1849 by the British government of India, was also brought by Katkov to Moscow. Afghani and Dalip Singh reportedly worked together for a possible revolt in India against the British.[43] Afghani wrote articles and gave interviews to Moscow newspapers containing criticism of British activities in Turkey, Iran and Afghanistan.

August, 1887. Arrived in St. Petersburg. Correspondence with certain Iranian high officials for removing misunderstandings about him. Nāṣiruddīn Shāh arrived in St. Petersburg on his way to

Europe in 1889. Afghani failed in his attempt to get a positive response from the Shah. Became more critical of Iranian policies. Afghani left Russia for Europe in the middle of 1889.

Munich, (1889)

Met the Iranian Prime Minister who sent Afghani back to Russia to explain to the Russian officials the circumstances in which certain concessions (that is, establishment of a national bank, rights of navigation in the river Karun, etc.) were given to Britain, an act which was resented by Russia. Afghani held talks with the Russian official and got certain proposals for the Iranian government. Left for Tehran.

Tehran, (Nov., 1889-91)

The Prime Minister did not see him regarding the outcome of the mission. After a while the Russian Govt. due to the delay, withdrew their commitments to Afghani and, on the other hand, the Iranian Prime Minister also expressed his non-involvement in Afghani's mission to Russia. The Shah and the British disliked his further stay in Iran. Afghani turned against the Shah, held secret meetings with the '*Ulamā* and the youth for the removal of despotism and for a constitutional government.

Was ordered to leave Tehran in July, 1890. He took refuge in the shrine of Shah 'Abdul 'Azeem and from there continued his attacks on the Shah. Was arrested and taken to Turkish border in January, 1891.

Early 1891

Expelled to Basra by the Ottoman government. Wrote a letter to the Iranian Mujtahid, Ḥāji Mirzā Ḥasan Shirāzi, against the Tobacco Concession granted by the Shāh to Imperial Tobacco Corporation owned by Britain, which played a vital role in the launching of a mass movement led by the Iranian '*Ulamā* against the Concession which was ultimately cancelled.[44]

1892, London

Arrived in autumn. Wrote articles in *Qānūn* (edited by Prince Malkam Khān, ex-Minister of Iran in Britain) and other journals against the Shah and Iran government.[45] Met E.G. Browne. Invitations from Sultān 'Abdul Ḥamīd to visit Istanbul through intermediaries, from February, 1892.

1892—1897: Instanbul

Arrived in the summer of 1892. Received with due respect by the Sultan and the Turkish religious elite. Was surrounded by Turkish and Iranian intellectuals and reformers including 'Abdul Qādir al-Maghribi, Muḥammad Pāshā Makhzūmi (who later published his *Khāṭirāt* based on Afghani's views, recorded during this period), Mirzā Āqā Khān Kirmāni, Shaikh Aḥmad Rūḥi, Ibrāhīm al-Muwailihi, 'Abdullah Nadīm of Egypt, etc. His main activity, encouraged and supported by the Sultan, was to implement his scheme of *Waḥdat al-Islāmiya*, by writing letters to the '*Ulamā* of Muslim countries, particularly of Iran. Stepped up his campaign against the Shāh of Iran. The Shāh was ultimately killed by Mirzā Riḍā Kirmāni, a disciple of Afghani, on May 1, 1896.

Afghani's relations with the Sultan deteriorated due to Afghani's uncompromising political views and his association with the revolutionaries. This was further aggravated due to the animosity of Abul Huda, an important religious leader, who accused Afghani of holding heretical views. A chance meeting between Afghani and the visiting new *khedive* of Egypt, 'Abbās Ḥilmi, in Istanbul in the summer of 1895, gave rise to the suspicion that Afghani, despairing of the Sultan, was working for the latter's Caliphate. Fallen from grace, he was kept under watch. Tried to leave Istanbul and seek British protection but failed. Died on March 9, 1897.

References

1. *Risālah*, p. 2; *Ta'rīkh*, i, pp. 27ff; *Mashāhīr*, ii, pp. 52-54; Shakeb Arsalān, *Ḥāḍir al-'Ālam al-Islāmi*, i (Cairo, 1343 A.H.), pp. 199-200; *Zu'amā*, pp. 60ff; 'Abd al-Raḥmān al-Rafi 'i, *'Asr Ismāīl*, ii (Egypt, 1932), p. 150; Maḥmūd Qāsim, *Jamāl al-Dīn al-Afghani* (Egypt, n.d.), pp. 9ff.; Sh, p. 100; Ghulām

Jīlāni A'zami, *Majallah-i-Kābul* (Kabul, July 7, 1931), pp. 21ff.; *Āthār*, p. 1ff.; Goldziher, *Encyclopaedia of Islam, art.* Djemal al-Din al-Afghani; General Nādir Khān, ex-king of Afghanistan, on the authority of Shakeb Arsalān and Mūsā Jārullāh, asserts that Afghani was an Afghan. He points out Afghani's appointment as the minister of Amīr A'zam as enough proof of his being a *Sunni* (written statement given to Qāḍi 'Abd'ul Ghaffār) *Āthār*, pp. 6-7. Ernest Renan, who met Afghani in Paris in 1883, describes him as "an Afghan" who "belongs to those energetic races of upper Iran bordering upon India, in which the Aryan spirit still persists." William G. Hutchinson, *The Poetry of Celtic Races and other Studies* (London, 1896), p. x; *Jarīdah-e-Muṣawwirah*, Maṭba' Thabāt, Istanbul, quotes Afghani, "I do not have any need to relate myself to any one nation (*millat*). I am an Afghan," *Āthār*, p. 19

2. For all such evidences and discussion on the subject, *Cf. Biography*, Chap. 2 and Appendix I.

3. *Millat*, Constintinople, *Tashrīn Īḥāni*, 1326/1926, quoted *Āthār*, pp. 18-19.

4. *Biography*, p. 428

5. For opinions supporting his stay in Iran, see *Biography*, Chap. 2, for opinions supporting his Afghanistan stay, see *Risālah*, pp. 2-3; *Mashāhīr*, ii, p. 53; E.G. Browne, op. cit., pp. 4-5

6. *Risālah*, p. 3

7. *Biography*, pp. 22ff.

8. *Risālah*, p. 2

9. A'zami, op. cit., pp. 31-32

10. *Biography*, p. 32

11. *Risālah*, p. 3. He also accompanied the Amir during his compaign against Herat in 1278/1861-62. ibid.

12. A'zami, op. cit., pp. 34-36

13. ibid. For Afghani's reference to Rafiq Khān, see Maḥmūd 'Ali Khān, *Ta'rīkh-e-Afghānistān*, Urdu translation of Afghani's *Tatimmah al-Bayān fi Ta'rīkh al-Afghan* (Lahore, circa 1342 A.H.), pp. 101, 104

14. *Risālah*, p. 5

15. *Biography*, pp. 32ff.

16. ibid., pp. 37ff.

17. *Documents*, p. 9

18. *Risālah*, p. 5

19. ibid., *Biography*, p. 4ff. for other sources.

20. *Risālah*, pp. 5-7; Browne, op. cit., pp. 6-7; *Biography*, ibid.

21. *Risālah*, p. 7.

22. Browne, op. cit., p. 7

23. *Risālah*, pp. 7; Jurji Zaidān, op. cit., ii, p. 56

24. Afghani's letter to a Turkish dignitory, written most probably during his stay in Egypt. *Biography*, pp. 129ff.; *Documents*, photos 26-27.

25. Maḥmūd Qāsim, op. cit., p. 26; Jacob M. Landau, *Parliament and Parties in Egypt* (Tel-Aviv, 1953), p. 86; *Zu'amā*, pp. 68-70.

26. Mahallati, op. cit., pp. 56ff.; *Risālah*, pp. 26ff.; *Al-Manār*, XI, p. 199

27. Statement of 'Abduh, quoted, SH, p. 491; *Zu'amā*, pp. 73-74; *Ta'rīkh*, i,

pp. 46-47; Maḥmūd Qāsim, op. cit., p. 40; Muḥammad 'Abd al-Fallāh, *Ashhar Mashāhīr Udabā al-Sharq*, i (Egypt, n.d.), pp. 45-46

28. Landau, op. cit., p. 82
29. W.S. Blunt, ibid.
30. *Zu'amā*, p. 76
31. *Risālah*, ibid.; Zaidān, op. cit., p. 57
32. For such criticism, *Cf.* Salīm Effendi 'Anhūri, *Ṣehr Hārūt*, (Damascus, 1303/1885), pp. 176-85. The author, however, withdrew his criticism when 'Abduh explained Afghani's religious outlook to him. *Risālah*, pp. 11-13; *Biography*, pp. 81ff.
33. For Afghani's impact on 'Abduh see Muḥammad 'Abduh, *Risālah al-Tawḥīd*, trans., B. Michel and M. Abdel Razik (Paris, 1925), Introduction; Charles C. Adams, *Islam and Modernism in Egypt* (London, 1933); A. Albert Kudsi-Zadeh, *The Legacy of Sayyid Jamal al-Din al-Afghani in Egypt*, unpublished Ph.D. thesis, Indiana University, Blommington, 1964; *Ta'rīkh*; Muḥammad 'Abduh, *Mudhākirāt al-Imām Muḥammad 'Abduh*, ed. Tāhir al-Tenali (Cairo, 1963), pp. 34-36; Ibrāhim Hilbāwi, "Ahamm Ḥadith Aththara fi Majrā Hayāti," *al-Hilāl*, XXXVIII, I, Dec., 29, pp. 138-40; Maḥmūdul Ḥaq, *Muḥammad 'Abduh : A Study of a Modern Thinker of Egypt* (Aligarh Muslim University, Aligarh, 1970), Chap. II; for various aspects, *Cf. Biography*, pp. 81ff.
34. *Risālah*, p. 8; W. S. Blunt, *Gordon at Khartoum* (London, 1911), p. 40
35. M, p. 88
36. W. S. Blunt, *India under Ripon* (London, 1909), p. 13
37. *Biography*, p. 184
38. ibid., pp. 213-14.
39. *Al-Manār*, VIII, p. 455
40. W. S. Blunt, *Gordon at Khartoum* (London, 1911), pp. 467-68
41. *Biography*, Chap. 9
42. For information on his visit to Iran and Russia, *Cf. Sharh*, pp. 39-44; Mahdi Malikzādeh, *Ta'rīkh-i-Inqilāb-i-Mashrūṭīyat-i-Irān*, Vol. I (Tehran, n.d.), p. 191; TBI, pp. 61-62; E.G. Browne, op. cit., pp. 42-43; *Biography*, Chap. 10
43. *Biography*, pp. 283ff.
44. For full text of the letter, *Cf.* TBI, pp. 68-71; *Tā'rīkh*, i, pp. 56-62; A summary with translation of important portions in E.G. Browne, op. cit., pp. 15-21; *Biography*, pp. 342-47.
45. Article, "The Reign of Terror in Persia", *Contemporary Review*, Feb., 1892; his interview in *Pall Mall Gazette*, Dec. 19, 1891; appeals Iranian '*Ulamā* to depose the Shah, *Ḍiyā al-Khafiqain*, London, Vol. 1, 1892; his letter known as *Ḥamalat al-Qur'ān*, addressed to Iranian '*Ulamā*, op. cit., March 1, 1892. For full text of the same, *Cf.* TBI, pp. 72-74; *Tā'rikh*, i, pp. 63-68; a summary appears, E.G. Browne, op. cit., pp. 24-26

SELECT BIBLIOGRAPHY

WRITINGS OF AFGHĀNI

Books and collections of articles :

Ḥaqīqat-i-Madhhab-i-Nīchari wa Bayān-i-Ḥāl-i-Nīchariyān, (Persian) First edition—Hyderabad, 1298/1881; Later editions—Bombay, *Muḥarram*, 1298/1881; Bombay, *Dhīqa'da*, 1298/1881; Tehran, 1303 Solar/1924-25. In Murtaḍa Mudarrisi Chahārdihi, *Ārā wa Mu'taqadāt-i-Sayyid Jamāl al-Dīn Afghāni*, Tehran, 1337/1958-59.

Translations :

Arabic

Shaikh Muḥammad 'Abduh, *Risālah fi Ibṭāl Madhhab al-Dahrīyīn wa Bayān Mafāsidihim wa Ithbāt anna al-Dīn Asās al-Madanīya wa'l-Kufr Fasād al-'Umrān*, Beirut, 1303/1885-86.

——, *Al-Radd 'ala al-Dahrīyīn*, another edition of the above with a preface by 'Uthmān Amīn, 2nd edition, Cairo, 1955.

English

In Nikki R. Keddie, *An Islamic Response to Imperialism : Political and Religious Writings of Sayyid Jamāl ad-Dīn "al-Afghānī"*, Berkeley and Los Angeles, 1968.

French

A.M. Goichon, *Réfutation des Matérialistes*, Paris, 1942.

Turkish

'Aziz Akpinarli, *Tabiatci'ligi Red*, Ankara, 1956. An earlier unpublished translation was made by Munir Effendi of Damascus and was seen and approved by Afghani. *cf. Orient*, vol. 12, Leiden, 1959, pp. 201-2.

Urdu
Radd-e-Nīcharīyat, Lahore, n.d.

Maqālāt-e-Jamālīya, (Persian).
First edition—compiled by 'Abd al-Ghafūr Shahbāz al-Bihāri, Calcutta, 1884, with the permission of Afghani. A collection of Persian articles written during his Indian visit and published in Indian journals, especially *Mu'allim* (Hyderabad) and *Mu'allim-e-Shafīq* (Hyderabad).
Later edition—compiled by Mirzā Luṭfullāh Khān Asadābādi and edited by Mirzā Ṣifātullāh Khān Jamāli, Tehran, 1312 Solar/ 1933-34. Contains additional articles besides those included in the above edition.

Urdu translation of the Tehran edition
Sayyid Mubārizuddīn Raf'at, *Maqālāt-e-Jamāl al-Dīn Afghāni*, Hyderabad, 1944. It wrongly ascribes certain couplets to Afghani (pp. 260-67). Their author is Mirzā Āqā Khān Kirmāni, the well-known Iranian nationalist. *cf.* TBI, pp. 140ff.

Al-'Urwah al-Wuthqā, la'nfiṣām lahā : Le Lien Indissoluble, Paris. Co-authored with Muḥammad 'Abduh.
First issue appeared on 15th *Jumādā* 1301 A.H./13th March, 1884, and the last issue on 26th *Dhu'l-Ḥijj*, 1301 A.H./17th October, 1884. In all, eighteen issues were published.
Published in one volume: 1st edition, Beirut, 1328 A.H./1920. Contains brief life-sketches of Afghani and 'Abduh by Musṭafā 'Abd al-Rāziq. Later, published several times. Latest edition, Cairo, 1958.
Reproduced in *Ta'rīkh*, ii, pp. 215 *et seq.*

Urdu translations of selected articles :
Sayyid Mubārizuddīn Raf'at, *Maqālāt-i-Jamāl al-Dīn Afghāni*, 1st edition, Hyderabad, 1946; 2nd edition, Karachi, 1952. Muḥammad 'Abd al-Quddūs Qāsimi, *Maḍāmīn-e-Jamāl al-Dīn Afghāni*, Lahore, n.d.

Tatimmah al-Bayān fi Ta'rīkh al-Afghān, edited and published by 'Ali Yusuf al-Kiridli, Cairo, 1901.

Urdu translation :
Maḥmūd 'Ali Khan, *Ta'rīkh-e-Afghānistān*, Lahore, circa 1342 A.H./1923. Introduction contains certain important information about Afghani's life.

Al-Waḥdat al-Islāmīya, Cairo, 1352/1933. Reproduced from *al-'Urwah*.
Al-Qaḍā wa'l-Qadar, Egypt, n.d. Reproduced from *al-'Urwah*.
Iraj Afshār and Aṣghar Mahdavi, *Documents inédits concernant Seyyed Jamāl-al-Dīn Afghāni* (*Majmū'eh-yi asnād va madārik-i chāp nashudeh dar bāreh-yi Sayyid Jamāl ad-Dīn mashhūr bi Afghāni*), Tehran, 1963. Contains a catalogue of Afghani's personal papers, left by him in Tehran in 1891.

Articles published in journals

Arabic
"Al-Ḥukūmah al-Istibdādīya," *Miṣr*, 11, 33, Feb. 15, 1879; reprinted in *āl-Manār*, Cairo, 111, *Rajab* 11, 1318/Nov. 4, 1900, pp. 577-582, *Rajab* 21, 1318/Nov. 14, 1900, pp. 601-607. Eng. tr. L.M. Kenny, "al-Afghāni on Types of Despotic Government," *Journal of the American Oriental Society*, 86, 1, 1966.
"Al-Sharq wa'l-Sharīqiyīn", *Abu Nazzara Zarqā*, Paris, VII, Feb. 2, 1883. Urdu tr. *Āthār*, pp. 193-205.
"Falsafah al-Tarbīya," and "Falsafah al-Ṣanā'a," *Miṣr*, Alexandria, *Jumādā* 5, 1296/April 25, 1879; reproduced in *Ta'rīkh*, ii, pp. 1-14.
"Al-Siyāsah al-Injlīzīya fi al-Mamālik al-Sharqīya," and "Asbāb al-Ḥarb bi Miṣr," *al-Manār*, XXV, March 25, 1925, pp. 756-760. Reprinted from *Tatimmah*.
"Al-'Illah al-Ḥaqīqīya li Sa'ādah al-Insān," *Miṣr*, 11, 20, Nov. 15, 1878. Reprinted in *al-Manār*, XXIII, Jan. 28, 1922, pp. 37-45.
"Bāb," in Buṭrus al-Bustāni, *Dā'irah al-Ma'ārif*, Beirut, 1881.

English
"An Afghan on the English," *The Bee/al-Naḥla*, London, Dec. 15, 1878.
"The Reign of Terror in Persia," *Contemporary Review*, Feb., 1892.

French
"Résponse ā Renan": A letter originally written in Arabic, the text

not available. French translation, *Journal des Débats*, May 18, 1883. Reprinted in A. M. Goichon, op. cit. Important passages translated in English, Muhammad Hamidullah, *Islamic Review*, London, May-June, 1958, pp. 33 *et seq*; *Biography*, pp. 189-195. A summary in Arabic, *Zu'amā*, pp. 89-93.

"Lettre Sur l'Hindoustan", *l'Intransigeant*, Paris, April 24, 1883. Reprinted in Elie Kedourie, *Afghani and 'Abduh : An Essay on Religious Unbelief and Political Activism in Modern Islam*, London, 1966.

"Le Mahdi," *L'Intransigeant*, Paris, Dec. 8, 11, 17, 1883. Reprinted in Elie Kedourie, op. cit.

"Pages peu connues de Djamal ad-Din al-Afghani," tr. Mehdi Hendessi, *Orient*, 6, 1958.

"Pages choisies de Djamal ad-Din al-Afghani," tr. M. Colombe, *Orient*, 21-24, 1962; 25, 1963.

"Les Anglais en Egypte," *La Justice*, Paris, March 27, 1883.

CONTEMPORARY AND SECONDARY SOURCES

Arabic

'Abd al-Fattāḥ, Muḥammad Ḥasan *Ashhar Mashāhīr Udabā' al-Sharq*, vol. II, Egypt, 1303 A.H.

'Abduh, Muḥammad, Foreword to the Arabic translation of Afghani's Persian treatise on the refutation of materialists, Cairo, n.d.

Adīb Isḥāq, *al-Durar*, Beirut, 1909.

Āghā Buzurg al-Tehrāny, *Ṭabaqāt A'lām al-Shī'a*, Najaf, 1373 A.H./1954 A.D.

Aḥmad Amīn, *Zu'amā' al-Iṣlāḥ fi 'Aṣr al-Ḥadīth*, Cairo, 1947.

'Anhori, Salīm Effendi, *Sehr Hārūt*, Damascus, 1303 A.H./1885 A.D.

Aṣma'i, *Āthār Jamāl al-Dīn al-Afghāni*, Egypt, 1901.

Farīd Wajdi, *Dā'irat al-Ma'ārif al-Islāmīya*, vol. 7., No. 3, Cairo, 1906.

Madkūr, 'Abd al-Salām, *Jamāl al-Dīn al-Afghāni, Bā'ith al-Nuhḍat al-Fikrīya fi'l-Sharq*, Cairo, 1937.

Maḥmūd Qāsim, *Jamāl al-Dīn al-Afghāni, Ḥayātuhu wa Falsafatuhu*, Egypt, n.d.

Al-Maghribi, 'Abd al-Qādir, *Jamāl al-Dīn al-Afghāni*, Egypt, 1947.

Makhzūmi, Muḥammad Pāsha, *Khāṭirāt Jamāl al-Dīn al-Afghāni al-Ḥusaini, Bā'ith al-Nuhḍat al-Islāmīya fi'l-Sharq*, Beirut, 1931.
Musṭafā 'Abd al-Rāziq, Preface to *al-'Urwah al-Wuthqā*, Cairo, 1928.
Al-Najjār, 'Abd al-Ḥalīm, *Madhāhib al-Tafsīr al-Islāmi*, translation of Goldziher's *Die Richtungen der Islamischen Koranauslegung*, Egypt, 1374 A.H./1955 A.D.
Qadari Qal'aji, *Jamāl al-Dīn al-Afghāni*, 2nd edn., Beirut, 1952.
Al-Qaṣṣāb, 'Abd al-Muḥsin, *Dhikr al-Afghāni fil-'Irāq*, Baghdad, 1945.
Al-Rāfi'i, 'Abd al-Raḥmān, *'Aṣr Ismā'īl*, vol. 2., Cairo, 1932.
Rāif Khouri, *al-Fikr al-'Arabi al-Ḥadīth*, Beirut, 1943.
Rashīd Riḍā, *Ta'rīkh al-Ustadh al-Imām al-Shaikh Muḥammad 'Abduh*, vol. 1, Cairo, 1931, vol. 11, Cairo, 1344 A.H.
——, *Tafsīr al-Qur'ān al-Ḥakīm*, vol. 4, 3rd edn., Cairo, 1365 A.H., p. 280; vol. 5, 1st edn., 1328 .A.H, p. 177.
Shakeb Arsalān, *Ḥāḍir al-'Ālam al-Islāmi*, vol. 1, Cairo, 1342 A.H.
Zaidān, Jurji, *Tarājim Mashāhīr al-Sharq fil-Qarn al-Tāsi' 'Ashr*, vol. 11, 3rd edn., Cairo, 1932.

Persian

Furṣat al-Dawleh Shirāzi, *Dīwān-i Furṣat*, Tehran, 1338 Solar.
I'timād al-Salṭanat, Muḥammad Ḥasan Khān, *al-Ma'āthir wa'l-Āthār*, Tehran, 1306 A.H./1881-89 A.D.
Murtaḍā Mudarrisi Chahārdihi, *Zindagāni wa falsafa-i-ijtimā'i wa Siyāsi-i-Sayyid Jamāl al-Dīn Afghāni*, Tehran, 1334 Solar.
——, *Ārā' wa Mu'taqadāt Sayyid Jamāl al-Dīn Afghāni*, Tehran, 1337 A.H.
——, *Khāṭirāt Sayyid Jamāl al-Dīn Asadābādi, Ma'rūf beh Afghāni* (tr. of *Khaṭirāt Jamāl al-Dīn al-Afghāni al-Ḥusaini*, by Muḥammad Pāshā Makhzūmi), Tabriz, 1328 Solar.
Nāzim al-Islām Kirmāni, *Ta'rīkh Bedāri-i-Irāniyān*, Iran, n.d.
Shaikh Muḥammad Maḥallāti Gharawi, *Guftār-i-Khush-i-Yār Quli*, Najaf, 1340 A.H.
Ṣifātullāh Jamāli Asadābādi, *Isnād wa Madārik Irāni al-Aṣl Budan Sayyid Jamāl al-Dīn Asadābādi*, Tehran, n.d.
Yaḥyā Dawlatābādi, *Ḥayāt-i-Yaḥyā*, Tehran, n.d.

Urdu

Abd al-'Ali, M, *Ḥayāt Nāṣiruddīn Shāh-i-Irān*, Delhi, 1897.

'Abd al-Ghaffār, Qāḍi Muḥammad, *Āthār-i-Jamāl al-Dīn Afghāni*, Delhi, 1940.

——, *Jamāl al-Dīn Afghāni*, Delhi, 1932.

Barni, Ḍiyā al-Dīn Aḥmad, *Jamāl al-Dīn Afghāni*, 1st edn., Delhi, 1924; 2nd edn., Karachi, 1954.

Nawāb Dhu'l-Qadar Jang Bahādur, *Sayyid Jamāl al-Dīn Afghāni*, Hyderabad, 1940. The article is included in *Maqām-i-Jamāl al-Dīn Afghani.*

Qāsimi, 'Abd al-Quddūs, *Maḍāmīn-i-Jamāl al-Dīn Afghāni*, Lahore, n.d.

Qāḍi Aḥmad Miyān Akhtar Jūnāgadhi, *'Ilm aur Islam*, translation of the lectures of M. Mismir and Ernest Renan on Islam and Science, from the original French, Azamgarh, 1934.

Raf'at, Sayyid Mubāriz al-Dīn, *Maqālāt-i-Jamāl al-Dīn Afghāni*, Urdu translation of Afghāni's treatise on the materialists and certain articles of *al-'Urwah*, Karachi, 1952.

——, *Maqām-i-Jamāl al-Dīn Afghāni*, collection of articles on Afghāni's life and mission by distinguished Indian scholars, Karachi, 1948.

Riḍā Hamadāni, *Jamāl al-Dīn Afghāni*, Lahore, 1956.

Zafar 'Ali Khān, *Jamāl al-Dīn Afghāni*, Lahore, n.d. This article is included in *Maqām-i-Jamāl al-Dīn Afghāni.*

Zafar 'Umar, *Mustaqbil-i-Islam*, tr. of the third chapter of *Western Culture in Eastern Lands*, by A. Vambery, Agra, 1910.

English

Abdul Hamid, Khwaja, *Ibn Miskawaih, A Study of his Al-Fauz al-Asghar*, Lahore, 1946.

Adams, C.C., *Islam and Modernism in Egypt*, London, 1933.

Ahmad, Aziz, *Studies in Islamic Culture in the Indian Environment*, Oxford, 1964.

Ameer Ali, *The Spirit of Islam*, London, 1953.

Amin, 'Uthman, *Muhammad 'Abduh*, Washington, 1953.

Antonious, George, *The Arab Awakening*, London, 1945.

Baljon, J.M.S., *The Reforms and Religious Ideas of Sir Sayyid Ahmad Khan*, Leiden, 1949.

Blunt, Wilfrid Scawen, *Secret History of the English Occupation of*

Egypt, Being Personal Narrative of Events, London, 1907.
——, *India under Ripon : A Private Diary*, London, 1909.
——, *Gordon at Khartoum*, London, 1912.
——, *My Diaries, Being a Personal Narrative of Events*, 1888-1890, London, 1932.
Browne, E.G., *Materials for the Study of the Bābī Religion*, Cambridge, 1908.
——, *The Press and Poetry of Modern Persia*, Cambridge, 1914.
——, *The Persian Revolution*, Cambridge, 1910.
——, *The Persian Constitutional Movement*, London, 1918.
——, *A Year Amongst the Persians*, Cambridge, 1927.
——, *Literary History of Persia*, 2 vols, London, 1951-52.
Burry, J.B., *A History of Greece*, London, 1956.
Donaldson, D.M., *Studies in Muslim Ethics*, London, 1953.
Edib, Khalide, *Conflict of East and West in Turkey*, Lahore, 1935.
Fazlur Rahman, *Prophecy in Islam : Philosophy and Orthodoxy*, London, 1958.
Fern, Vergilius, *An Encyclopaedia of Religion*, London, 1956.
Ferriman, Duckett, *Turkey and the Turks*, London, 1911.
Gibb, H.A.R., *Modern Trends in Islam*, Chicago, 1945.
——, *Whither Islam*, London, 1932.
Graham, C.F.I., *Life and Works of Syed Ahmad Khan*, London, 1885.
Heyd, Uriel, *Foundations of Turkish Nationalism*, London, 1950.
Heyworth-Dunne, James, *Religious and Political Trends in Modern Egypt*, Washington, 1950.
Holt, P.M., Lambton, K.S. and Lewis, Bernard, *The Cambridge* History of Islam, vol. 2B, Cambridge, 1970.
Hutchinson, William G., *The Poetry of Celtic Races*, London, 1896.
Iqbal, Muhammad, *Six Lectures on the Reconstruction of Religious Thought in Islam*, Oxford, 1934.
Karpet, Kemal H., *Turkey's Politics, The Transition to a Multi-party System*, Princeton, 1959.
Keddie, Nikki R., *An Islamic Response to Imperialism : Political and Religious Writings of Sayyid Jamāl ad-Dīn 'al-Afghānī'*, Berkeley & Los Angeles, 1968.
——, *Sayyid Jamāl ad-Dīn 'al-Afghānī', A Political Biography*, Berkeley, Los Angeles and London, 1972.
Kedourie, Elie, *Afghani and 'Abduh, An Essay on Religious Unbe-*

lief and Political Activism in Modern Islam, London, 1966.

Lambton, Ann K.S., *Secret Societies and the Persian Revolution of 1905-6*, New York, 1959.

Landau, Jacob M., *Parliament and Parties in Egypt*, Tel-Aviv, 1953.

Layard, Austin Henry, *Nineveh and its Remains*, vol. 11, London, 1849.

Levy, Reuben, *The Social Structure of Islam*, Cambridge, 1957.

Mahmudul Haq, *Muhammad ʻAbduh : A Study of a Modern Thinker of Egypt*, Aligarh Muslim University, Aligarh, 1970.

Molt, J.R., *The Muslem World of Today*, London, 1925.

Nejla Izzeddin, *The Arab World*, Chicago, 1953.

Nuseibeh, *The Ideas of Arab Nationalism*, New York, 1956.

Palgrave, W.G., *Essays on Eastern Questions*, London, 1872.

Ramasaur, E.E., *Young Turks, Prelude to the Revolution of 1908*, New Jersey, 1957.

Sharif, M.M., ed., *A History of Muslim Philosophy*, Wiesbaden, 1963, 1966, 2 vols.

Smith, Wilfred Cantwell, *Islam in Modern History*, Princeton, 1957.

Stoddard, Lothrop, *The New World of Islam*, New York, 1921.

Thilly, Frank, *A History of Greek Philosophy*, New York, 1948.

Vambery, A., *Western Culture in Eastern Lands*, London, 1906.

Watt, W. Montgomery, *Free Will and Predestination in Early Islam*, London, 1948.

——, *The Faith and Practice of al-Ghazali*, Cambridge, 1957.

Zenkousky, Serge A., *Pan-Turkism and Islam in Russia*, Cambridge, 1960.

(For additional sources and articles, see bibliography of *Biography*).

INDEX